Tourguide
to the
Rocky
Mountain
Wilderness

Cover color photo, other photographs and maps
by author.

Tourguide
to the
Rocky
Mountain
Wilderness

by Raymond Bridge

Stackpole Books

TOURGUIDE TO THE ROCKY MOUNTAIN WILDERNESS

Copyright © 1975 by
Raymond Bridge

Published by
STACKPOLE BOOKS
Cameron and Kelker Streets
Harrisburg, Pa. 17105

Printed in the U.S.A.

Library of Congress Cataloging in Publication Data

Bridge, Raymond.
 Tourguide to the Rocky Mountain wilderness.

 1. Rocky Mountain region—Description and travel—Tours.
2. Hiking—Rocky Mountain region. 3. Camp sites, facilities, etc.—Rocky Mountain region. I. Title.
F721.B74   917.8'04'3   75-9885
ISBN 0-8117-2036-5

Other books by Raymond Bridge
THE COMPLETE SNOW CAMPER'S GUIDE
AMERICA'S BACKPACKING BOOK
FREEWHEELING: THE BICYCLE CAMPING BOOK

Contents

Introduction

THIS IS A book for wilderness lovers who are planning camping trips to the Rocky Mountains south of Canada. It is not an introduction to the Rockies as a whole, though some of the trips suggested in this book would provide a fine introduction. To discuss the entire Rocky Mountain region would require an encyclopedia or a series of broad generalizations. There are literally tens of thousands of miles of trails in each of most of the states in the area, and no one person can have hiked more than a small fraction of them. TOURGUIDE TO THE ROCKY MOUNTAIN WILDERNESS provides information on a few selected spots in each of the Rocky Mountain states. Hopefully, the reader will be able to visit and come to know some of these areas, any one of which could be explored for weeks on end.

One of the purposes of this book is to try to provide visitors seeking a wilderness experience with an alternative to the most popular and overused parts of the Rockies, particularly the National Parks. In choosing the areas discussed an attempt has been made to choose places that do not get excessive use. Overconcentration in particular areas is one of the main causes of environmental deterioration in the Rockies. Thus, the reader will not find any discussion here of trails in Rocky Mountain National Park, which receives floods of visitors every year, simply because it is a National Park and is colored green on everyone's road map. National Parks have generally been avoided in this book for that reason. The only exception is the coverage of the northwest corner of Glacier National Park, which is well-secluded from the vast numbers of people zooming over the Going-to-the-Sun Highway.

An attempt has been made in this book to provide information that will be useful to all those with a love for the wilderness, whether they are family car-campers who take occasional hikes from the campgrounds, ambitious backpackers who like to go hard for a week at a time, or those who fall somewhere in between. It is a book, however, for those who like their country unspoiled. There is no listing of suburban campgrounds, complete with amusement parks, swimming pools, and pinball machines, perched by the sides of superhighways. Though many attractive campgrounds are listed, facilities are likely to consist of picnic tables, fireplaces, and pit toilets. They are chosen mainly as adjuncts to the country around them—rivers, streams, lakes, and mountains.

In each of the areas discussed in the book, various trips are recommended ranging from easy hikes to backpacking jaunts that would normally be of several days duration. Some attempt is made to give the reader an idea of the length and difficulty of the various walks, though it is never possible to do this with complete accuracy, because individuals will vary so much in their abilities. After taking a few of the hikes listed in the book, the reader should have some idea how his or her own hiking speed and feelings about difficulty relate to the descriptions in the recommended trips.

The first part of the book includes some descriptive information about the Rockies, which may be useful and interesting to

The foothills of the Rockies have many beautiful trails, too. This one is near Boulder, Colorado, in a city park.

those who are not well-acquainted with the Range. The Rocky Mountains cover a vast region in North America, one which is naturally somewhat difficult of access. The terrain, wildlife, climate, and ecology vary tremendously, even in that part of the Range within the contiguous United States. The brief description included in this book can only touch on some of the variety of the mountains. The more time one spends in these mountains and plateaus, the more obvious it becomes that our knowledge is still very limited.

Several chapters are included giving recommendations on camping techniques for the Rocky Mountain High Country. Those who are experienced in camping there may want to skip these chapters altogether and proceed to the section on suggested trips. Longtime campers from other parts of the U.S. or Canada might simply want to skim them briefly to note differences between the Rockies and their own home ground, while beginners should spend some time looking this part of the book over before they set out for the mountains.

One of the attractive aspects of the Rockies is their combination of a great deal of true wilderness with ready accessibility. They are not remote, bad-weather mountains which can only be approached using expeditionary techniques and with the endurance of great hardship. There are few locations even in the most remote parts of these mountains that cannot be reached by a hike of two or three days from some roadhead or other. Past mining and ranching activity has left a network of access roads which allow the visitor with only a short vacation to get a real taste of the country.

Convenient as it is for the tourist, this system of roads poses a real threat to the land, particularly to those parts that are still wild, for there is no great buffer zone of roadless foothills to protect the mountains from the spoilers. It is up to those visitors who care for the country to preserve it. They must use it lightly, attempting as much as possible not to leave signs of their passage, and sometimes removing reminders left by others. Equally important, they must remember that there is a limit to how easy access can be without destroying what people come to see. Put another way, there are enough roads and there is more than enough pavement right now to get everyone to the edge of the backcountry that wants to visit either its edge or its interior. Every bit of additional road that is laid, every winding road widened into eight-lane superhighway, merely destroys another part of the wild and beautiful land that is the property of all Americans.

It is the primary purpose of this book to help people who like to visit and enjoy some of the most beautiful country left on the face of the earth. It is the hope of the author that after you have visited some of these places, you will help to preserve them.

-i

The Rocky Mountains

THE GREAT CHAIN of the Rocky Mountains, extending all the way from central Alaska to the southwestern United States, forms part of a great mountain divide which continues on through the rest of the Americas to the south. Within the contiguous United States, the portion of the Range which is the province of this book, the Rockies form the backbone of the North American continent, dividing the watersheds of the Atlantic Ocean and the Gulf of Mexico from those of the Pacific.

On a large scale, the pattern formed by the Rockies is fairly simple, its high, broken crest rising out of the Great Plains to the east, often lifted above the prairie below by over 9,000 feet in a few miles. To the west, the Rockies drop off into the high plateau of the Great Basin between them and the Pacific Cordillera.

A more detailed look at the country, however, reveals a considerably more complex picture. The Rockies, themselves, are made up of many smaller chains, trending in various directions, often with large bowls, basins, and parks intervening. At places the range is interrupted, and the country becomes temporarily quite flat. There are also a good many mountain ranges throughout the Great Basin, and it is not always easy to say where the Rockies stop and the "intermountain area" begins.

At the northern end of the Rocky Mountains in the contiguous U.S. is Glacier National Park, which forms a part of the Waterton-Glacier International Peace Park together with its Canadian counterpart to the north. The Continental Divide passes through the Park, which lies entirely in Montana. The mountains and the terrain here are reminiscent of the Canadian Rockies to the north, though the glaciers here have largely disappeared. The huge stratified mountains rise above steep, forested slopes and beautiful lakes that are often over ten miles long. Though the highest peaks are only 10,000 feet above sea level, the mountains are actually as large as much higher peaks to the south, because they rise from relatively low elevations. The mountains of Glacier are some of the most beautiful in the United States, and some parts of the Park are not at all crowded.

South of Glacier National Park, the Rockies along the Continental Divide become lower and more rounded. There is beautiful country here in the Bob Marshall Wilderness, but the more spectacular peaks at this latitude are to the west in the Bitterroot Mountains, which run for many miles along the Idaho-Montana border. Eventually the Divide joins the Bitterroots at the headwaters of the Salmon River. There are many lesser ranges on both sides of the crest in Montana and northern Idaho.

In the corner where Montana and Idaho meet Wyoming is Yellowstone National Park, and on its eastern border is the fascinating Absaroka Range. At this latitude, though the mountains are not at all continuous from east to west, there is a series of great and spectacular ranges over an east-west distance of fully 500 miles. To the east of the Absarokas and slightly south are the Big Horns, and occupying the same position to the west are the Tetons. Still further west, in Idaho, are the magnificent Sawtooth peaks. This series of uplifts includes some of the most beautiful

Looking across the high peaks and out onto the plains. There are more worlds to explore here than can be touched in any one lifetime.

scenery in the Rockies, and it also includes a wide variety of mountain moods. Where the Absarokas are largely volcanic, the Tetons are formed from a hard and durable granitic gneiss. Where the Tetons are fully visible from nearby roads, a visitor has to walk long distances to get a good view of the Big Horns.

South of the Tetons are some small ranges, and then for over a hundred miles stretches the great alpine wilderness of the Wind River Range. Beyond the Wind River mountains there is a major interruption in the spine of the Rockies in southern Wyoming. The Continental Divide even splits here for some distance, so that those few drops of water which fall between the two crests simply find their way into the Great Divide Basin, rather than moving towards one of the oceans. The main crest of the Rockies resumes further east, and begins rising towards the great uplifts in Colorado.

It is in Colorado that the Rockies of the contiguous U.S. reach their climax. Of the 72 peaks between the Canadian and Mexican borders which reach 14,000 feet or more above sea level, Colorado has 54. There is a score of different mountain ranges within the state, and a lifetime would not suffice to begin exploration of their peaks and valleys. The mountains have great variety as well: there are stratified peaks resembling those of the Canadian Rockies and the mountains of Glacier National Park, and there are vertical walls of glacially polished granite. There are dark, brooding crags and ranges of light rivalling John Muir's Sierra. There is lush forest and parched desert. When one climbs to a high summit in one of the other Rocky Mountain states and sees a distant range of mountains, it is usually easy enough to identify, while in Colorado the sea of peaks is often so vast that orientation is hard.

Farther west, other links of the Rocky Mountain chain extend into Utah. The most important mountains are in the northeast corner of the state, in the Wasatch and Uinta Ranges.

South of Colorado, the mountains again begin to drop off in altitude and to become less continuous. The highest mountains in New Mexico are in the extension of the Sangre de Cristo Range which extends south from Colorado, but scattered chains of peaks, sometimes very rugged, extend all the way to Mexico.

The Great Barrier

This huge network of peaks, valleys, lakes, rivers, forests, and parks has been one of the most important geographical features of the North American continent for millions of years. It has formed a barrier influencing the movement of storms and men. It is the home of many species of animals and plants. The headwaters of many of the great rivers of the Continent rise in the Rockies. The mountains provided hunting grounds and homelands for many Indian tribes, and later they were a temporary refuge for some of the native Americans fleeing west from the relentless pressure of the European colonists. White trappers, explorers, and mountain men found the Rockies to be an inexhaustible source of beauty, adventure, and furs.

For most settlers moving west from the growing United States, however, the Rockies constituted the Great Barrier, impeding their progress toward the new promised lands in the Pacific region. The Great Plains were home for many and provided easy travelling for late-comers, but few were enticed by the Rockies themselves. For the pioneer driving his wagon across the grasslands, the first sight of the jagged peaks rising up out of the plains ahead signalled the start of the real hardships. The important geographical features for the settler heading west were the passes, the low sections of the mountains which allowed the easiest passage. Most such passes and the trails linking them were used by the Indians for millenia before the arrival of the Europeans. They became known and developed by the Whites as the mountain men worked through the Rockies, trapping and trading furs. For pioneers heading west, the most important of these passes was South Pass, which crosses where the Rocky Mountain chain is interrupted in southern Wyoming.

The Gold Rush

The first big rushes for gold were to California, and the Rockies at this time were a barrier again, but it was not long before discoveries of precious metals in the Rockies themselves lured tremendous numbers of immigrants. Various discoveries in the 1850s and 60s suddenly made the mountains desirable to fortune seekers from around the world, and together with increasing agriculture and the building of the railroads, sealed the fate of the Indians living in the region.

The Colorado Rush of 1859 alone brought some 100,000 people into the Rockies, and ultimately settlements and roads were pushed into the most unlikely crannies of the high country in the quest for precious metals. The building of the railroads through the Rockies consolidated the settlement that had been begun by gold.

The People

The history of the Rockies has resulted in great diversity among the people who live there. Many Indians still live on some reservations where the land has not become sufficiently desirable to their neighbors to force another repetition of their tragic history. Still other Indians have moved into the mainstream culture. Many Mexican-Americans still maintain their own cultural traditions, particularly in the southern part of the Rockies, which were once a part of Old Mexico. Men from all parts of Europe were attracted by the search for gold, and later by ranching, sugar beet culture, and other types of agriculture and mining. Chinese laborers were imported to work first in the mines and then on the railroads, and many stayed. Japanese came to work on farms, and finally the most recent wave of immigration began a few years ago when hundreds of thousands of people from other parts of the United States began to move into the Rocky Mountain region to try to escape urban problems and crowding in the areas where they had previously lived.

A Visual History

The events described briefly above and many others are quite apparent to the observant traveller in the Rockies. Both modern roads and backcountry jeep tracks generally follow the same routes that were used by previous generations, because those paths followed the lines of least resistance through a rugged terrain. Many parts of the Rockies have easy access only because the lust for gold and silver (and later uranium and other miner-

An afternoon hike along an easy Rocky Mountain trail. Note that there are rules governing household pets in many areas, to prevent their disturbing wildlife. If you plan to take your dog, avoid National Parks and check the rules in advance elsewhere.

als) gave men the incentive to punch roads through exceedingly difficult country.

Many of the richer parts of the mountains are literally honeycombed with mine shafts. Depending on the area and on one's mood, these old diggings may be fascinating tourist attractions, ugly scars on the land, or melancholy reminders of the past. The observant traveller in these mountains will find constant reminders of times past, however. Almost every time one drives to a high campground well up in the mountains, it will be an old mining road—sometimes improved, sometimes not—that one follows. Even a modern with the most cynical attitude about the lust for gold and its long-term effects cannot help developing a grudging respect for the tenacity and courage of the men who built some of these roads.

Those parts of the mountains which are still difficult of access, with long trail approaches and no roads, are generally those where the search for precious metals proved fruitless. Ranges like the Wind Rivers in Wyoming are the more precious to us now, because they retain their true wilderness quality and are approachable only on their own terms.

Many other aspects of the history of these mountains are apparent to the visitor also. The railroad grades snake along the canyons, sometimes with tracks above still visible where Chinese laborers trotted. The ruins of ancient native civilizations are spectacular and provocative, and the remnants of nomadic cultures can also be found by observant wanderers. Those who are interested enough to read local history before or during a trip will be rewarded with a good many insights into both the country and the people who came before.

CHAPTER 2

Car Camping
in the Rockies

CAR CAMPING IS simply staying outdoors at campsites acces-
sible by road with equipment that may range from a sleeping bag
thrown out on the pine needles to elaborate mobile homes. From
the campground one may go fishing, take hikes of a few hours,
leave on a backpacking trip, or simply sit and enjoy the surrounding countryside. This type of camping is particularly suitable for families not accustomed to rugged wilderness trips or to
those who want a relaxed vacation that will give them a taste for
the great variety that the Rockies offer.

The art of this type of camping is in being comfortable and at
home through any sort of weather with a minimum of cumbersome equipment and with little or no impact on the environment.
Experienced car campers will have little or no trouble when they
come to the Rockies, and for them this chapter is intended mainly
to point out the conditions they should expect in the mountain

states. Beginners may wish to whet their skills on a few weekend trips close to home before starting on a long camping trip in the high country.

Clothing

Though the climate of the Rocky Mountain region is not nearly as severe as many prospective visitors seem to expect, wide variations in temperature and weather do occur, particularly in the spring and fall. The mountains are fickle by human standards, and the change from a balmy afternoon to a raw, cold, wet one can occur with amazing swiftness. The higher the altitude, the more extreme and changeable the weather is likely to be. Because of this variety, it is well to have a wide range of clothing available. One may easily find heavy wool clothing to be a great comfort only a half an hour after lolling comfortably around in a bathing suit.

Most campers will bring whatever they have at home to meet such a wide variety of possible conditions, but to avoid having to carry the equivalent of a clothing store around the mountains, it is usually best to carry a number of light layers of clothing which can be worn one over the other, rather than trying to take large numbers of garments of different thickness.

The principle of dressing in layers is especially suitable for hiking, because it is easy to peel off a few pieces of clothing as the air loses its morning chill and activity warms your body. Removing extra clothing prevents the body from overheating, so that clothes that may be needed for warmth later on do not become sweat-soaked and cold.

Hikers should be careful to take enough clothing along with them, even on jaunts that are expected to last only a few hours. Cool mountain breezes can be quite chilling at lunch and rest stops, even though the sun feels quite hot when one is hiking along. The wind may also be blowing much harder in unprotected regions above treeline. Temperatures are usually colder as elevation is gained, and there is always the prospect of rapid weather changes in the high country.

Some clothing in the mountains should always be of wool or

of a synthetic substitute which retains some warmth when wet. Cotton garments are almost as cold to wear as bare skin when they become soaked by rain, whereas wool, bulked Orlon, and clothing insultated with Dacron, Fiberfill II, Polarguard, and the like retain a good deal of their warmth even when wet. Carrying clothes that retain insulating value after a soaking is important for comfort in an unexpected storm and for survival in an emergency situation.

A windproof outer garment is essential for anyone planning hikes above timberline and is worthwhile for even the casual camper. Strong winds are common in mountains everywhere, particularly in the Rockies. A fuzzy sweater will provide plenty of insulation with little weight, but only if a wind-tight shell prevents a gale of cold air from blowing right through.

A warm hat is one of the most valuable pieces of clothing one can carry to prevent the body from being chilled. Human beings are warm-blooded mammals, and their important organs have to be kept at a fairly constant temperature to function. In order to protect the organs in the trunk, the body will slow or completely stop circulation of warm blood to most of the extremities to reduce loss of heat. Thus, the hands and feet and most of the skin will become quite cold when a person is losing too much heat. Since the head has the most essential organ of all, however, warm blood will keep going to the head to supply the brain with oxygen even if the body is becoming dangerously chilled. Over half of the body's total heat production can easily be lost through the head alone if it is unprotected, so carrying a hat is particularly important for anyone who may encounter cold conditions—and that includes anyone camping and hiking in the mountains.

Comfortable, sturdy footwear is important to the camper. Exploring around camp, whether over great or small distances, provides a lot of the fun on a camping trip, and ill-chosen boots or clothing is likely to spoil a lot of it. Boots are usually best, particularly if one plans to do much hiking, but they need not be higher than ankle length. Fit is more important than style. The boot should be comfortable and roomy when worn over the socks that will be used. The toes should not be cramped, even when the foot is pushed forward (with the laces tight), but the heel should be reasonably snug. Feet swell somewhat on long walks, particularly if they are not in condition, and a boot that is tight at the beginning of a hike will be excruciatingly so by the end. A loose fit around the heel will cause blisters.

The soles of boots or other footwear shouldn't be too slippery, lest they be dangerous on rough trails, particularly in the rain. The best type of boot varies with the intended use and with individual preference. Sneakers are found satisfactory by some, but they provide little protection for the feet, get wet easily, and are not particularly recommended. Very heavy mountaineering boots are excellent for difficult mountaineering, but they are cumbersome, expensive, and uncomfortable for anything else; they should be avoided by casual hikers. Try to find comfortable walking boots in between these extremes.

Heavy wool socks or a synthetic substitute are best. Light socks will not protect the feet from chafing. Cotton socks rapidly become clammy and uncomfortable on a hike. One good combination is a pair of heavy "ragg" wool socks worn over a pair of light Orlon socks. The two pairs help to reduce blister-causing friction, and the soft inner pair prevents the wool from causing itching or irritation for most people.

Rain gear is essential for comfort in inclement conditions. Local thunderstorms are common in the Rockies, and they can build up in a very short time. Though such storms generally have a fairly short life, they can bring a lot of precipitation together with high winds during that span. Hence, though almost any rain garments will do for use around camp, hikers above timberline should consider durability and protection against the wind when they choose wet-weather clothes. Strong winds will often make short work of very lightweight plastic.

Shelter

The possibility of strong wind gusts should also be considered when choosing and setting up a tent or other shelter. Strong and well-made equipment will last longer, but careful use is probably more important. Pitching a tent sloppily will allow winds to whip it and exert tremendous shock forces. Flapping will in turn break loose stakes, guy lines, or seams, allowing still more slack to be caught by the wind, until finally the whole tent blows down or is ripped apart. It is thus a good idea to spend some time at home learning to put up one's shelter efficiently and well, and to get in the habit of always pitching it strongly. This way, when the time finally comes that the tent has to withstand strong winds, the occupants will not be forced out in the middle of a rainy night to try to keep it from blowing down.

Besides conventional tents, campers, tent trailers, and the like, many lightweight and inexpensive shelters work quite well in the Rockies. Tarps and tube tents are perfectly satisfactory if they are well-pitched, since long periods of continuous wet weather are quite uncommon in this part of the country. Thus, many campers who prefer to avoid expensive paraphernalia or who cannot afford it carry modest shelters and may sleep out under the stars when the weather is good. The effects of wind should be remembered, however, and taken into account. The greater the area presented to the wind, the stronger and better tied down the shelter must be. There have been many occasions when big wall tents have been blown down while little plastic tube tents nearby have easily weathered a storm.

Campers using tents should carry a couple of kinds of stakes, a set intended for normal ground and a handful of spikes for use when gravel pads masquerading as tent platforms are encountered. Even the owners of self-supporting tents should have stakes available to hold the tent down in windy weather.

Sleeping Bags and Beds

The nights tend to be cool in the Rockies even in the summer, and they are frequently cold in early spring and late fall. Sleeping bags should be adequate to keep their owners warm in these conditions. No hard and fast rules can be laid down, because both individuals and their equipment vary a good deal. Those using self-contained camping vehicles with heaters may be satisfied with sheets and light blankets, while campers sleeping out under the night sky will want reasonably warm

Relaxing at a subalpine campsite. The flowers and spectacular views make this kind of camp particularly pleasant. However, the environment at this altitude is fragile; use stoves instead of fires, and avoid areas which receive heavy use.

bags. Some people will need far more insulation than others, depending on their metabolism, whether they wear clothes to bed, how tired they are, and so forth. Thus, in buying a sleeping bag or choosing which one to take on a trip, consider your own body and the kind of camping you intend to do. The combination of sleeping bag and shelter should be adequate for temperatures of around freezing for camping in the higher parts of the Rockies. Remember also that excessively warm bags can be as uncomfortable as those that are too thin.

Tent campers should remember to bring some sort of ground bed as well. Most sleeping bags, particularly down-insulated ones, compress to negligible thickness under the weight of the body. For efficient use of the insulation of the bag, it is necessary to have a ground bed to keep the body off the cold ground. A majority of people also find sleeping directly on the hard ground to be rather uncomfortable, and beds of soft pine needles are not always at hand. Air mattresses or foam pads should be carried. Either is satisfactory, but most campers find foam pads more comfortable.

Cooking Utensils and Stoves

When car camping, visitors should restrict fire-building to existing fireplaces. This is generally legally required in the National Forests and National Parks discussed in this book. Use only dead wood which is already down, and do not build fires when the woods are extremely dry or when the wind is high. *Never* build a fire on forest duff (smoldering remains can stay alive for weeks beneath the surface and spring into flame long after you have gone) or leave a fire until it is drowned out and cold to the touch. Most forest fires are caused by careless campers. When the fire danger is highest, fires may be completely banned—there is good reason when this is done, and the regulation will be rigidly enforced, so obey it.

These cautions mean that the camper cannot always depend on cooking over a fire, pleasant as this might be. Hence, a portable stove should always be carried. There are many kinds available, and the choice is a matter of taste. Two-burner stoves operated on white gas or naphtha fuel have proved reliable and inexpensive to operate, and their size is a good compromise between compactness and versatility. Another good reason for carrying a camp stove is that heavy use of some campgrounds often depletes the supply of dead wood, particularly at campgrounds in arid regions or those near timberline. There is no excuse for disfiguring live trees for a campfire, so if wood is scarce, a stove is the alternative to a cold supper.

Fairly simple cooking utensils make camp cooking easier and more pleasant. If you are a novice, keep the menus simple as well. Seven-course meals should wait until one is comfortable with the conditions of camp cooking, and most experienced camp chefs avoid them anyway. Some of the older pots from the kitchen will do well enough if your budget is tight. If special cooking pans are going to be bought, avoid those made of thin aluminum unless they are being bought for backpacking as well as car camping. Thicker pans are less likely to burn the food when used over fires and gasoline stoves. Many campers like Teflon-lined pans for ease in both cooking and cleaning.

Stew-like main dishes greatly simplify planning and preparation of the menu, and they are likely to save money as well. Some sort of canned meat can be used with noodles, rice, and similar starches, and various vegetables and seasonings make this single dish a complete or almost-complete meal. Carry a dishpan to make cleaning up easier, and don't forget to spread the chores around the group. Trash, grease, and garbage must be burned or put in trash receptacles, never buried or strewn about the campground.

Water

Water is not generally too much of a problem in the Rockies, and most of the campsites listed in this book have supplies of safe running water. However, these may occasionally malfunction, a few campgrounds do not have them, and if some series of events forces one to camp at a roadside clearing, it is convenient to have enough water in the car for drinking and cooking. It is wise to carry a few gallons at all times.

Water taken from streams or lakes should always be boiled for five minutes or chemically treated before it is used for drinking. It may be used for cooking or washing dishes, of course, if it is boiled in the process. Never assume a stream is safe unless you *know* it is. Though many Rocky Mountain streams are safe, pollution has to be assumed even at quite high altitudes unless one is quite familiar with the country. In some areas, for example, sheep are grazed right up to the Continental Divide, and they can drop some rather unpleasant bugs into the water.

Bring enough water bottles or canteens to keep your whole group supplied during day hikes, fishing trips, and the like. Air at high altitude is often quite dry, particularly in the Rockies, and breathing this air combined with perspiring on the trail can drain the body of surprising amounts of moisture.

Spring and fall campers should not depend on campground water supplies. These are likely to be shut off sometime in September and drained so that freezing water will not burst the pipes, and they are not turned on until sometime in June or July at many campgrounds.

Seasonal Conditions

Temperatures in the Rockies in the summer are very pleasant on most days. The sun shines a good deal of the time, and most of the storms that do come up are local thunderstorms which pass as quickly as they arrive. Evening temperatures are pleasantly cool, even after very hot days. Some warm clothing should be carried, however, since bad weather can be cold, and at high altitude a freak storm can bring snow at any time of the year.

In the fall, occasional storms bringing heavy snow should be expected as a matter of course. The visitor will probably miss them, but they occur every year, and they can make life very miserable indeed for the unprepared. A couple of feet of snow can fall anywhere in the Rockies in September, though the weather will probably warm up again soon after. Thus, tire chains, a shovel, and cold weather camping equipment should

Those who are willing to head into the hills in winter reap their own rewards. These cross-country skiers, having spent the night in an igloo, are trying out the fresh powder snow.

always be carried on fall camping trips, and automobiles should be ready for cold weather since even without snow nighttime temperatures are likely to fall below freezing.

These same comments apply to the early spring trips. In the spring it is also important to check in advance on road conditions, since there is a great deal of variation in the opening time of roads closed by winter snows. Passes may be cleared in April one year and not until July the next. Where roads are closed, the visitor will find campgrounds under snow as well.

Winter conditions in the Rocky Mountain high country are as rugged as might be expected. Skis or snowshoes are generally needed for travel, and the beginning camper is not likely to consider the outdoors inviting for overnight stays.

All this should not discourage the prospective visitor from taking a camping trip in the Rockies during the off seasons. The fall and the spring have special rewards for anyone willing to put up with frosty mornings. The crowds disappear, and the air has a delicious tang. In the fall, if one is lucky enough to catch the aspen turning, there will be spectacular views of golden hillsides as the snows creep down from the slopes above. In spring, water cascades everywhere, and flowers begin poking tentatively up even before the snow has finished melting above them.

The winter is a particularly rewarding time for those who can cope with it. The Rockies make especially fine ski touring country, but the beginner will want to confine his trips to day tours at first. Snow camping can be exciting and comfortable, but it is not really suited for the neophyte outdoorsperson.

Planning a Trip

Perhaps the best advice that one could give to the first-time camper in the Rockies is not to try to see too much. There is a tremendous amount of spectacular and rugged terrain in this part of the country, but to develop a real understanding of and appreciation for it, one must get out and hike along the trails, smell the wild flowers, and sit beside streams swollen by melting snow from above. By trying to cover too much ground, it is easy to rush along the highway system, catching glimpses of many peaks while fighting traffic jams, without ever getting back into the heart of the mountains.

It is generally a better plan for those with normal vacation periods to visit a few areas or just one, allowing them time to really get to know it, to hike several trails or get in a long backpacking trip, to fish or watch birds, and to develop a real affinity for the chosen group of mountains. This plan also minimizes driving time and gas consumption, an increasingly important factor for everyone.

The maps and descriptions included in this book should enable the reader to pick a relatively uncrowded itinerary which is compatible with the skills and wishes of the party. In each area a variety of trips is suggested, ranging in difficulty from very easy to rather long and strenuous. Each hike is also likely to suggest others, once familiarity with a spot begins to grow.

There is enough information in the book for casual hikers, but it is always a good idea to get a set of topographic maps for any area where one plans to hike and camp extensively. The main reason is that the condition of trails varies a good deal from year to year. New ones are cut, and old ones become overgrown, though this process is slower in the Rockies than in many parts of the country. More importantly, even the best of guidebooks will sometimes be ambiguous and confusing. A rocky spot where a trail becomes hard to see will seem obvious to one person, while it is very hard for another to follow. Spring snows may cover a long enough section of trail to cause the hiker a lot of difficulty. With a topographic map, physical features are clearly shown, and the way can be found even when the trail is not apparent.

For those who do not know how to read topographic maps, the argument for always having them along is even stronger. Knowing how to use them in conjunction with a compass is an essential skill for outdoor people, and there is no more effective or painless way to learn than to carry along a map on moderate hikes, stopping occasionally to correlate the contour lines and other symbols on the map with the physical features in one's surroundings. After the novice has taken a few hikes using this plan, the technique of map reading will begin to be clear.

If several areas are to be visited, it is usually wiser to pick a group in the same general region. The distance between the northernmost and southernmost campgrounds discussed in this book is well over a thousand miles by road, and anyone trying to visit them both on a two-week vacation will spend most of the time driving.

Those who are unfamiliar with rough mountain terrain and high altitudes should be conservative in making plans. Many people need time to acclimatize to higher altitudes and are not able to go on long hikes immediately after getting to a campground at 9,000 feet above sea level, particularly if the hike involves a lot of scrambling over steep trails. Children and novices are particularly likely to become unhappy if they are pushed along on an excessively ambitious schedule. Allow for rest days and rainy periods in estimating how much country can be covered in a limited amount of time.

Planning the menu in advance can save a good deal of time and trouble on the trip. Stores in small mountain towns may be expensive and may not be open when you come through. Carrying all the food for the trip, prepacked in bags for each day, or at least having a shopping list ready for a supermarket along the way will allow the camper to avoid wasting time and money hunting out supplies.

Carry a good suntan lotion on all hikes as well as in the car. Much less ultraviolet light is filtered out by the atmosphere at high altitudes, and severe burns can result from the sun in the mountains, even on cloudy days. Be particularly wary of reflection off the snow; it can burn places which are not normally exposed and have no protective tan, such as the area under the chin and the bottom of the nose. Good sunglasses should be carried for all members of the party for the same reason, to prevent sunburn of the eyes (snow-blindness).

Insect repellent should be part of your camping supplies. The Rockies are not as bad as many areas in breeding biting bugs, but there is an ample supply of the pests some times of the year.

CHAPTER 3

Backpacking in the Rockies

THIS CHAPTER CANNOT really serve as an introduction to the sport of backpacking as a whole. Subjects like cooking, boot selection, sleeping bags require whole chapters or books of their own, and novices who have not done any backpacking before would be well advised to consult one or more of the many books on the subject, such as the author's *America's Backpacking Book.** All that can be covered here are the special characteristics of the Rockies which make backpacking there different from the Appalachian Trail, the Sierra, or the Minnesota woods.

The Rockies are an ideal playground for the backpacker. There are thousands of miles of trails and countless more thousands of miles of excellent off-trail backpacking routes. Throughout much of the range, vegetation is sparse enough, particularly at high alti-

* (See also *Home In Your Pack* by Bradford Angier; *Introduction To Backpacking* by Robert Colwell available from Stackpole Books.)

tudes, to permit the experienced hiker to choose his own route. Glaciation has left a strong enough mark to satisfy the most accomplished mountaineer, but these mountains are old enough and the glaciers are sufficiently receded so that the backpacker and scrambler can find moderate routes to the tops of most peaks without having to resort to the skills and equipment of the technical mountain climber (ropes, crampons, nuts, pitons, etc.).

Most parts of the Rockies get enough precipitation so that one is not forced to carry unmanageable loads of water for drinking, yet summer rains are more often afternoon showers than steady rainstorms setting in for days at a time. Thus, while the backpacker must needs be equipped for occasional wet weather, long and continuous periods of soaking are uncommon.

Clothing

The section on clothing in the preceding chapter covers most of the subject, but backpackers should pay particular attention to the vagarity of Rocky Mountain weather in making their plans. At high altitudes, the sun can be quite hot, but snow is possible during any month of the year. Worse yet, wet cold weather accompanied by heavy winds may be encountered at times, and improperly clothed hikers will quickly find their bodies' reserves of warmth will be drained away in such conditions. Hypothermia (dangerous chilling of the core of the body) can kill the unwary backpacker caught in such circumstances, and the victim is often unaware of his or her danger. Proper clothing, periodic snacks to provide the body with fuel, and attention to chilling—whether in your own case or noticed in your companions—are essential.

The main emphasis in choosing clothing should be on a number of layers, including some sweaters or shirts made of wool or a synthetic substitute which maintains some of its insulating quality when wet. Rain gear and shell clothing to keep out the wind are important, and so is a good, warm hat. A light hat with a brim is also needed in the hotter and more arid parts of the range, as in parts of New Mexico.

Footwear is critical for backpackers who must carry their

A backpacker on the trail early in the morning. The stunted trees are quite old—life is a tenuous thing in this harsh environment.

homes on their backs and everything on their feet. The trails in the Rockies tend to be rugged, and most people will find that their feet will become bruised and sore if they wear light shoes. Reasonably heavy hiking boots will protect the feet from stones. It is helpful, particularly in the spring, if they can be made reasonably waterproof with one of the standard wax treatments. (Only boots made of full-grain leather, not split leather, can be made at all watertight.) More treatment should be used when wet conditions are expected, and less when conditions are dry, since in the latter circumstances it is best to let the boot breathe, so that perspiration can escape.

The soles of the boots should have good traction, to prevent slips. Those planning to travel a lot on snow may want fairly heavy boots to allow step-kicking. Heavy wool socks are standard, usually with a pair of lighter wool or Orlon liners. Fit is most important of all. The body of the boot should be roomy, but the fit, with heavy socks, should not be sloppy, particularly at the heel, or bad blisters will be raised. The toes should not hit the boot when going down a steep hill. Boots should be broken in *before* the trip.

Sleeping Gear

A warm, lightweight sleeping bag is probably the most important piece of equipment for backpacking in the Rockies. One can survive without one, but very few people can sleep comfortably with thin bags, blanket rolls or similar contrivances, particularly above timberline. All-night warming fires, which were the means used by a lot of old-timers to get through the chilly nights, are no longer permissible in these days of shrinking wilderness and expanding population.

Unfortunately, good sleeping bags are awfully expensive, so if you are buying one rather than renting or borrowing, be sure to get one that is well-made and adequate to your needs. Down bags are the lightest for a given amount of warmth and will stuff into the smallest space in your pack. Close-cut bags using Polarguard and Dacron Fiberfill II are less expensive and less affected by moisture. Construction and quality materials are the most important factors, however. Spend some time checking the catalogues or shops of reputable mountaineering suppliers before you spend a lot of money on a bag, particularly a "bargain." Make sure you consider your own characteristics before picking a bag. If you tend to sleep "warm," needing fewer blankets than most people to be comfortable and relishing open windows on chilly nights, you may be able to get by with a lighter bag than most. If, on the other hand, you tend to sleep "cold," you may need a heavier bag than the average backpacker. You must take the seasons you intend to use the bag into account. Remember also that temperature ratings used by different suppliers are only roughly comparable; one manufacturer's 20° bag will be another's 5° bag.

All materials used to insulate sleeping bags for backpackers are quite compressible—they have to be if the bag is to be both warm and portable. Thus, the insulation under the body will be squashed very thin unless it is made of a different material than the bulk of the bag. This squashed material will allow the body to lie almost directly on the cold, hard ground. For this reason, a backpacker generally carries a short air mattress or foam pad to support the body from the shoulders to the hips, using clothing and packs for a pillow and to pad the legs and feet. Foam pads, though somewhat more bulky, are warmer and more suitable for most people than air mattresses.

Tents and Other Shelters

Experienced backpackers have a wide range of opinions on the most suitable shelter for backpacking in regions like the Rockies. Probably the most commonly used equipment is the two-man mountain tent, a sophisticated and expensive development of the old pup tent, normally having a sewn-in waterproof floor, an uncoated nylon roof, and a separate waterproof fly which pitches over the tent. Well-made mountain tents give excellent protection from all sorts of weather, can be pitched even on snow or above timberline with impunity, and will withstand fierce winds. There are similar, larger tents for groups and families.

Less expensive versions of these tents, made of a permeable material that will shed a good deal of rain, such as cotton-nylon mixtures, can be very satisfactory. If they are well-made, they can be used in all the situations already mentioned. More commonly, cheaper tents are made with a single layer of coated nylon fabric. Such tents are unsuitable for cold weather, but they can be very satisfactory for camping in spring, summer, and fall, providing one takes good care of them. They are normally not as well constructed as the most expensive mountain tents, so they are best pitched in reasonably sheltered spots, out of the worst of the wind. Condensation on the inside of the roof of one of these tents will be a real problem. Getting as much ventilation as possible will help, as will avoidance of cooking inside, particularly when meals require a lot of boiling.

Tarps and tube tents can also be used quite successfully for backpacking in the Rockies, since the rain in most areas is sporadic rather than continuous. More care must be used in choosing sites and in pitching the shelter correctly against the wind, but for those who enjoy going with a minimum of equipment and weight and those with limited budgets, such shelters are a good solution. Tarps should be sturdy to withstand winds—lightweight plastic sheets are not usually satisfactory. With tube tents, a few clothespins of the spring type will allow the ends to be partially closed against wind-driven rain.

Lean-tos and other shelters built completely or partially of boughs have no place in this region, since the resulting environmental damage is unsightly and would be quite severe if many users engaged in the practice.

Stoves and Fires

For both practical and environmental reasons, anyone backpacking in the Rockies should carry a small stove and fuel. The wood supply at many high-altitude campgrounds is insufficient for cooking fires, so those who do not carry stoves may have difficulty in some areas. More important, trees in sub-alpine zones grow very slowly. Tiny, gnarled timberline trees may be hundreds of years old. The backpacker's ideal should be to leave his campsite in as good a condition as it was found (or better), so that succeeding campers will not even know he was there. Only if all visitors follow this practice can the land stand heavy recreational use, so that we can avoid the need for bureaucratic regulation of access. Confine your fires to well-wooded lower altitudes, preferably where fireplaces already exist.

When building fires, use only dead wood which is already down, so as not to scar the campsite. Don't build a fire when there is a lot of wind or when the woods are extremely dry. Build the fire on a mineral base which is clear of debris for some distance around. If you must build your own fireplace, it is helpful to cover the stones with mineral soil, so that they will not be fire-scarred when you leave—carbon blacking will last for centuries as an unpleasant reminder of your passage. Obviously, fires should never be left unattended and should be out dead cold when you leave. Stir the remains and drown them until they are cold to the touch.

Other Equipment

Except in the driest parts of the Rockies, a quart water bottle is generally adequate. Water purification tablets should be carried and used, unless you are quite sure the water is pure in the area where you are backpacking. Sheep graze at fairly high elevations in some parts of the mountains. In the North Park Range, for example, they can be found right up on the Continental Divide. Pack trains of horses may cause problems elsewhere.

Sunburn lotion and good sunglasses or goggles are important, particularly in spring, when there is still a lot of snow to reflect sunlight. At high altitudes it is much easier to get a burn or to have the eyes injured by excessive sunlight because there is less atmosphere above to filter out ultraviolet radiation.

Insect repellent will sometimes make life on the trail much more bearable. The most effective repellent for the weight is the

Looking up at a peak towering above from a rough trail. Those who want to avoid pack trains will get away from them quite quickly on routes like this.

one containing the largest percentage of N, N-diethyl-me-
tatoluamide.

Planning A Trip

If one has not done a lot of backpacking before, it is important to start planning well ahead of time, making up lists of all
the equipment that will be needed, so that nothing will be forgotten in the last minute rush. The maps in this book show particular routes, but it is best to carry topographic maps of the
area where one is walking. The specific topographic maps
published by the U.S. Geological Survey which cover each area
discussed in this book are listed in the appropriate descriptions
of backpacking routes.

In deciding the distance that can be covered in a day, it is
wise to be conservative. Those who have not done any lengthy
trips at high altitudes should be particularly wary of expecting
to cover a lot of rugged terrain over 9,000 feet each day. Allow
an easy day or two to begin acclimatizing to the altitude. It is
also prudent to allow for a couple of days a week (at a
minimum) for bad weather or for just resting, wandering about,
and looking at the scenery. Ten miles per day with a couple of
thousand feet in altitude gain is a good rate of travel for most
experienced and strong backpackers with loads for one- or two-
week trips. Beginners should plan on half that distance, while
the very strong and ambitious may go quite a bit farther. It is
well to remember, however, that doing fifteen or twenty miles
with several thousand feet of climbing is much harder to manage
day after day than it is on a single weekend. Whatever the level
of experience and condition of the party, longer distances can be
managed on good trails that are fairly flat, perhaps half again
the distances mentioned above. If there is a great deal of
climbing or rugged cross-country travel expected, cut the distance planned in half.

On long trips. food for a couple of extra days should always
be carried for safety and comfort, particularly if the trip is such
that there is no way to shorten it if progress is slower than ex-

Camping in the high country in spring and early summer is especially exhilerating, but if the roads have just opened, be prepared for a lot of snow around. This bicycle camper has picked a spot near a stream swollen with spring runoff.

pected. Carry food that has proved satisfactory in the past; long trips are bad times to test unproven (and possibly unpalatable) menus. Beginners should be particularly wary of buying a lot of packaged meals with which they have had no experience. The numbers of people which are supposedly served by some freeze-dried meals are apparently determined more by creative marketing men than by any realistic experience in the field. Novices should try out their proposed meals at home first. It is also important to allow for increased appetites on the trail. Backpacking burns a lot more calories than sitting at a desk.

A good deal of care should be taken in choosing routes that are commensurate with the experience and ability of the weakest members of the party. It is easy to bite off more than one can chew in the exuberance of planning the trip. It is even easier for the planner, who is generally the strongest member of the party, to bite off more than other participants with more modest appetites will be able to enjoy. Most people have fun on trips that are well within their physical ability. If a real bash is being contemplated, it should be with the understanding of the whole group.

Getting maps, schedules, food, and equipment planned and put together well in advance is one of the most important guarantees of a successful trip, particularly for the relatively inexperienced. Desperate last minute attempts to get equipment and information are exhausting at best, and essential items are often forgotten as a result of such scrambling.

Those planned excursions at high altitudes in spring should be careful in choosing routes. A good deal of snow will still be found in the high country early in the season. Camping and hiking in such conditions can be very rewarding, particularly since the mountains then are most beautiful, but difficulties will be increased. Depending on circumstances, progress may be quite a bit slower, and dry campsites may be hard to find. Water will not be a problem, since meltwater will be found everywhere, but the nights will be quite chilly. Good gaiters to keep snow from getting into one's boots will be essential.

The most important caution for those planning spring trips, and sometimes early summer ones, is to beware of steep snow

Steep snowfields are common in the high country at any time of the year. They may be easily climbed, but a slip can send the unwary hiker sliding down at a great rate. Snowfields are particularly dangerous as they become harder during the summer. Stay clear of long, steep slopes and those leading to dropoffs, unless you have an ice ax and the knowledge of how to use it.

slopes where a slip could be dangerous. Kicking steps up such slopes is often quite easy in spring conditions, but mountaineering skills are often necessary to provide safety. Before risking a climb up or down a snow slope, consider the consequences of a slide—if they would be serious, it is best to turn back unless the party is equipped with ice axes and the skills to use them properly.

Rocky Mountain Expeditions, Inc.

This organization offers a variety of interesting *escorted* trips in the Rockies, ranging from backpacking to bicycle and ski touring—even custom trips. Their brochure is available by writing:

Rocky Mountain Expeditions, Inc.
P.O. Box 576
Buena Vista, Colorado 81211

CHAPTER 4

Natural History

THE ROCKIES MAKE a particularly rewarding region for the observation of natural forces and processes at work, especially for the camping vacationer spending time in or around wilderness regions. There are no places in the contiguous United States which have not been affected in a major way by human incursions, but many of the areas discussed in this book have been changed far less than most parts of the country.

There is a great deal to be learned here by any thoughtful observer, whether he or she is a long-time student of some fields of natural history or a complete novice. Many aspects of the natural sciences are far more apparent in this land of contrasts than they are elsewhere. Geologic forces and the results of their action over the millenia are apparent all around. The changes in life zones as one travels from slopes with an eastern exposure to those facing west, or as one moves up or down in altitude, are apparent to the most casual onlooker. An afternoon hike can bring the visitor to a variety of plant and wildlife communities that would be equalled only by days of automobile travel to the north in flatter country.

This chapter introduces some of the natural history of a vast region and suggests a few books that may take the visitor a bit farther than he can be guided through these few pages. From there it will be easy to go on as far as he likes, whether the study is to add some additional interest to one trip or to become an avocation of a lifetime.

Geology

As with most great mountain ranges, the geology of the Rockies is very complex. Most of the kinds of geologic activity have their examples somewhere in this massive uplift, and sifting them out, one from the other, is difficult enough for the professional geologist. The amateur, unless he or she is particularly dedicated, must usually be satisfied with looking at and understanding some of the more obvious features.

As a whole, the Rockies are a middle-aged mountain range. They are considerably younger than the Appalachians, for example, and as a result they are higher and more rugged because the forces of erosion have had far less time to wear them down and round them off. They arc, however, quite a bit older and more worn than the Cascades of the Northwest, and the terrain is consequently less rugged than in the Cascades.

The region now occupied by the Rockies has had a long history of rises and falls in elevation, and as a result there are complex patterns of rocks, some thrust up from deep in the earth where they once melted and later cooled, some having exploded from the depths in volcanic eruptions, some washed down by streams from earlier mountains and later bonded together, and some deposited on the bottoms of ancient seas.

For hundreds of millions of years this region moved up and down. When an uplift occurred, the forces of erosion would sculpt the land, cutting valleys and washing away some deposits.

A typical glacial cirque. A glacier carved out of these cliffs and left the rocks it had carried down when it melted. The valleys of many Rocky Mountain streams lead to cirques like this, often with lakes at the bottoms. It is often impossible to exit at the top of the cirque without mountaineering skills and equipment.

When the land sank, material would be carried in and deposited in layers that were sometimes miles thick.

The most recent surface depression came in the Cretaceous period. Some earlier rises and falls had involved only part of the Rocky Mountain region, but this time the entire area was covered by a great sea, which stretched from the Gulf of Mexico to the Arctic Ocean. This submergence began perhaps 135 million years ago, and thick layers of sedimentary rocks were deposited at the bottom of the sea. Gradually, in the period less than one hundred years ago, a new uplift known as the Laramide Revolution began. The sea was rolled back. The great underlying block of granitic rocks formed 600 million years ago was pressed up under the sedimentary layers above, bending them upwards like a great dome. This upthrust created most of what are now known as the Southern Rocky Mountains, and the core of these granitic rocks is often visible in the high peaks of this region, occupying much of Colorado and portions of New Mexico, Utah, and Wyoming. The edges of some of the upthrust layers of sedimentary rock are visible in many places along the edge of the range.

These great disturbances form complex patterns, everywhere slightly different. As an upthrust occurs, streams carry down sediments to form new bands of rock along the edges of the uplift, and these may be lifted and eroded in turn. As the earth's crust is bent and broken, molten rock spews forth from fissures, forming volcanoes. Like the sedimentary rocks, these volcanic deposits may be eroded away to become part of the debris washed down to the foothills, or they may be strong enough to stand above the surrounding eroded area, forming high peaks. Some plugs of molten rock did not reach the surface, but filled cracks below, cooled and hardened, only to be exposed later as the surrounding material was carried away. Water flowed through some cracks, became laden with minerals in the superheated depths, and escaped to the surface where the minerals were deposited.

Folds were created by the upthrust as tremendous pressures were exerted on the surface, and the crust of the earth buckled and rippled. In the area which is now Glacier National Park, the crust

The ancient history of the mountains is written in the rocks. This pinnacle in the foothills is formed from layers of sediment that were deposited on the floor of a sea that once covered much of what is now the Rocky Mountain region. The layers of deposition are clearly visible slanting down from the top of the rock down to the right. When the mountains rose, these layers were tilted up at their present angle along the front of the range, and weaker rock around was eroded away to leave this spire.

was first folded, and finally one whole section thrust up over the layers next to it. This overriding portion, called the Lewis Overthrust, later eroded to become the Lewis Mountains.

Elsewhere great blocks were lifted up where a fault formed because of the strains to which the surface of the earth was subjected. The Teton Range in Wyoming was formed by such a fault block.

All these varied uplifts have subsequently been eroded by water running off them and carrying away weaker layers. They have been carved by great masses of ice during periods of intense cold. The glaciers in the U.S. Rockies have now receded to reveal the piles of rock they carried down to their bases (moraines) and the great semicircular bands of cliffs they carved and smoothed (cirques). The glaciers themselves are now quite small in the few spots where they have not melted away completely, but the evidence of their tremendous power remains where they have scooped out valleys and shaped mountains.

Some parts of the Rockies received little or no glaciation, and the higher parts of these sections form either rounded mountains or high tablelands, segmented here and there by deep river valleys. Where the land has continued to rise, rivers have sometimes cut tremendous canyons and gorges, such as the Royal Gorge of the Arkansas and the Black Canyon of the Gunnison, both in Colorado.

Climate And Weather

Most mountain ranges have weather which is very changeable and climate which varies a great deal, even over quite short distances, and the Rockies are no exception. Mountains interfere with the flow of major weather systems and may intensify their activity, but the effects in the mountains, themselves, are likely to be quite different on the leading and trailing sides, or in the valleys as opposed to the peaks. Mountains also create their own weather, and the final mixture of weather and climate that results is complex.

The weather systems affecting the Rocky Mountain region generally move in from the Pacific and since they pass first over

Precipitous scenery above some high Rocky Mountain lakes. The carving of these cliffs demonstrate the power of glacial action.

the Coast Ranges, they lose most of their moisture there. The land between the Coast Ranges and the Rockies is thus extremely dry. Because so much moisture has already been sucked from the air masses before they reach the Rockies, this Range is much drier than those closer to the Pacific, and water is therefore a precious commodity in the Rocky Mountain States. The mountains are so high, however, that air passing over them cools a great deal, and since cold air can carry less moisture than warm, the Rockies often manage to extract some precipitation even from relatively dry air. The western slopes of the mountains tend to receive most of the moisture, since the air is cooling as it rises over those slopes, while the eastern slopes tend to be drier.

Since the mountains form a major barrier to the movement of air masses coming from the west, there is a great deal of turbulence around the peaks when a weather system is moving through. Large amounts of air may be pushed through small gaps, and extremely high winds may result. Some parts of the Front Range in Colorado are renowned for their high winds, particularly in the winter. Such winter winds may be very cold or they may warm as they descend in altitude and are compressed, producing a *Chinook*, a warm winter wind that may raise the air temperature fifty degrees in a few hours.

In summer, one of the most common phenomena of Rocky Mountain weather is the afternoon thunderstorm. Particularly strong updrafts are often produced among the peaks because sunlight striking the mountainsides directly, even from a low angle in the morning, warms them rapidly, and the nearby air, which is also warmed, rises. Such updrafts may be fairly gentle or extremely turbulent, depending on how they combine. If there is enough moisture in the air, thunderheads form, sometimes rising to tremendous heights. When lightning results, the tops of the mountains make excellent lightning rods, as do any hikers who happen to be standing there.

One of the main characteristics of the climate of the Rockies is the change in temperature which occurs as one climbs in elevation. By going up a thousand feet one finds very similar temperature changes to those one would discover by travelling several hundred miles north, and there are similar effects on the kinds of plants and animals which can live in an area. Because of the effect of cooling on the air that may move through, gains in elevation in many parts of the Rockies also correspond to increases in the amount of precipitation that can be expected. In a typical part of the Range, if one travels up into the mountains from the high plateau on the west, one will move from hot desert into cool and wooded slopes, and finally to places where snow remains much of the year.

Life Zones

The climatic changes which occur with changes in altitude result in variations of the plants and animals that are to be expected. Wherever one travels in the world, one will find typical plant and wildlife communities. Certain types of forest are dominant in New England, for example, and they develop in certain ways. Within a particular kind of woods, one will normally find certain birds and animals; in a meadow one will find others, and along a river bottom still others. In the mountains, one has the additional dimension of altitude.

It has already been stated that the climate as one moves uphill in the mountains tends to resemble that found at more northern latitudes, and so do the communities of plants and animals. Thus when one walks up a mountain in Colorado, the vegetation and animal life around will be seen to change in a way similar to the way they would as one travelled much greater distances to the north on level ground. The parallel is not perfect, but it is amazingly close.

At lower altitudes on either side of the Rockies, the climate is likely to be quite dry. The grasslands of the Great Plains extend along the eastern slope of the range. Vegetation, soil, and climate are more variable on the western side, ranging from true desert to sagebrush and grassland zones.

As one goes slightly higher, one will move through transition zones, which may include various types of brush and small trees, such as piñon pine, juniper, or mountain mahogany. The main transition zone, often known as the foothills zone, is dominated

The mood of the mountains changes with the weather and the seasons. Winter in the Rockies.

by scattered stands of Ponderosa pine, which requires less moisture than many of the trees growing higher up. Douglas fir becomes more and more mixed with the Ponderosa as one moves higher and continues into what is commonly called the montane zone. Depending on various factors, one may also find cedar, hemlock, Colorado blue spruce, lodgepole pine, aspen, and other trees in this zone. Higher still are the subalpine forests, the most typical trees of which are Engelmann spruce and subalpine fir. Where forests have been temporarily destroyed by fire, avalanche, or wind, aspen and lodgepole pine will take over first. Stands of limber and bristlecone pine may be found. At the limit of the trees, there may be little groves of gnarled old whitebark pine.

The highest zone, above timberline, is the alpine zone, a region of small, hardy plants, which can survive the harshest conditions and reproduce in the very short growing season available to them. The tundra of this zone is very similar to that found in the arctic.

Naturally, there are many variations in the pattern, which has been presented here only in a rudimentary way. Other trees appear in the forests; there are meadows and bogs; vegetation in rainy areas is different than in dry ones, and the range of species in Montana is not the same as in New Mexico. Still, the similarities in the orderly progression as one moves from low altitude to high are striking.

Animal life changes along with the plants on which it depends. The black-cap chickadee gives way to the mountain chickadee with increasing altitude, and the house finch is replaced by Cassin's finch, and finally on the peaks themselves by the rosy finches.

Some animals remain always in a particular zone. The marmots and pikas which squeak or whistle at the hiker as he walks over an alpine rockfield remain there throughout the year, but the elk that may cool himself in summer by rolling in a nearby snowbank will retreat to lower elevations when the snows come. Some birds may migrate thousands of miles away, some never go far, and some will temporarily retreat down the mountainsides to escape an occasional severe storm.

Early summer in the high country. This summit can be reached by a good trail, giving a panoramic view of the country below. The climber in the foreground has just ascended by a more difficult route.

There is a great variety of wildlife to be observed in the Rockies, particularly in wilderness areas, some kinds easy to find and some difficult, some quite common and some extremely rare. The presence of man has had a disastrous impact on a number of species and very little on others. The grizzly bear is now nearly extinct in the contiguous United States, where he was once master in much of that country. The coyote, on the other hand, despite earnest attempts at his destruction, has managed to scorn his human enemies. Most commonly, it is the destruction of the environment on which animals depend for their food which has diminished their numbers, though deliberate hunting has devastated some species.

Studying The Natural History Of The Rockies

The main difficulty faced by the average camper trying to understand some of the country around him is deciding where to begin. The ideal way is to take an experienced naturalist along to explain things as one lolls around a campfire or strolls along a mountain trail. There is no easier way to learn the names and habits of birds painlessly or to develop an understanding of the geology of a mountain and its surrounding valleys. Such tours are often available in the National Parks, but most people trying to visit uncrowded areas will have to rely on their own resources. They will have to depend on a few books to help them get started.

Often the best source of information is a guide which discusses a particular limited area, giving a basic summary of its geology, climate, and topography, and listing some of the common plants and animals with notes on identifying them. Such guides can dispense with a great deal of extraneous information and can thus concentrate on just what it is that the tourist may want to know. This type of guide is usually available for National Parks, either as a single book or a series. Visitors to Glacier National Park, for example, can pick up a series of booklets on the geology, mammals, birds, and other interesting features of the Park by stopping at one of the visitor centers before heading for one of the more distant corners of Glacier.

Most of the areas discussed in this book, however, are not covered by such convenient publications.

The most common plants and animals of the Rockies are presented very well in two small books published by the Naturegraph Company of Healdsburg, California. They are *Wildlife and Plants of the Southern Rocky Mountains* and *Wildlife of the Northern Rocky Mountains*, the first covering the area roughly from Colorado, south, and the second from Wyoming, north. They cover all the mammals in which the beginner is likely to be interested, together with some of the plants and birds.

Birds are one of the most easily visible and interesting types of wildlife for the casual visitor to identify. The best field manual is *Birds of North America* by Robbins, *et al.*, published by Golden. Those new to birding, however, should start practicing their identifications at home. Skill at recognition of basic bird forms and habits takes some cultivation, and first attempts to use a manual are likely to be thoroughly frustrating on a short vacation.

The companion Golden manual on trees is also excellent, *Trees of North America* by Brockman, *et al.*

The wildflowers of the Rockies are one of their most attractive features, for they bloom in profusion from early spring into the fall, often covering whole mountainsides with carpets of color. They tend to be difficult to identify, however, despite the fact that they will stand still for the observer, because there are so many varieties. Picture books without any keys usually cover far too few species to be very useful. This means that unless one has a knowledgeable person along, it will be necessary to learn how to use the guide book with some botanical terms and keys to have a very high success rate at identifying flowers. There are three good guides to the regions which are fairly complete and are intended for amateurs. Each has some advantages, and none can be recommended over the others without qualification. They are: *A Field Guide to Rocky Mountain Wildflowers* by Craighead, *et al.*, Houghton Mifflin; *Handbook of Rocky Mountain Plants* by Nelson, D.S. King, Publisher, Six Shooter Gulch, 875 W. Cresta Loma Rd., Tucson, Arizona; and *Rocky Mountain Flora* by Weber, Colorado Associated University Press. The last concentrates mainly on Colorado.

The United States Geological Survey, besides publishing topographic maps, also publishes maps showing the geology of particular regions and various pamphlets and papers on the subject. Lists of the available material on a particular area can be obtained by writing to the Survey, at the address listing for obtaining maps, and requesting information. Though these materials are aimed at professional geologists, if the interested layman orders them in advance of a trip and spends some time deciphering the terms used with a geology textbook, he will be able to make good use of the information later on when hiking about.

INTRODUCTION TO SPECIFIC TRIPS AND AREAS

THE REST OF this book is comprised of recommendations of specific places to visit and information about hikes and backpacking trips that can be taken in each of these areas. A few words are in order about the format and the best way to use the accompanying information.

Campgrounds are discussed in connection with each area, and most of them are chosen so that hikes can be taken directly from the campground, so that no additional driving is necessary. In a few places there are no suitable campgrounds near the best trailheads, and if so this fact is mentioned. The number of sites at each campground is listed. Unless there is information to the contrary, all these campgrounds have water available, but it is prudent to carry a little water in the car in case faucets or pumps are not operating. In spring and late fall it should be assumed that water will be shut off.

There is a map included in each section which shows the hikes and backpacking trips in the region, and I have tried to prepare these carefully from all available information, including U.S.G.S. maps, Forest Service maps, and my own experiences and observations. The amount of ground covered is very large, and I am sure there are some mistakes and ambiguities, for which I apologize. In each case where they exist, I have included a listing of the U.S.G.S. maps which cover each trip.

These can be obtained by mail from the Distribution Section, U.S. Geological Survey, Federal Center, Denver, Colorado 80225. At the time this is written, prices are 75c each, postpaid, for any 7½' or 15' map listed in this book. For any lengthy trips, particularly in more remote regions, topographic maps are recommended.

Trails are shown on the maps in this book by dotted lines, and roads, paved or dirt, are shown by double solid lines. Roads that may not be passable with normal passenger vehicles are shown with double dotted lines. Depending on the scale of the particular map, trails other than those described may or may not be shown. When cross-country routes are described, they are shown on the map with crosses.

The number of days or hours that will be required for a trip is not listed, because it was felt that these tend to be misleading. Hikers vary so much in their abilities and inclinations that one person's day hike may be a four day backpack for another. Mileages and elevation gain give an objective picture of the major factors that affect the length of time that a trip will require. Experienced backpackers will already have a good idea how much ground they can cover, and beginners should be able to find out what their level of skill and ambition is after trying a couple of hikes. Divisions have been made between hikes and backpacking trips at an arbitrary level, in order to group different treks into longer and shorter walking tours, but those who want leisurely backpacking trips may often find suitable ones listed as hikes, while tigers can pick day hikes from the backpacking sections. Where other factors, such as brush, rough trails, or stream crossings may significantly affect hiking speed, these are usually mentioned in the trail description.

A wide variety of mountains are described in this book, and the visitor should be able to find some suitable places by reading some of the descriptions. There are regions of deep wilderness described here that do not lend themselves to family car camping and day hikes. Others are perfect for these purposes but have little to offer the wilderness traveller looking for a trip to last several weeks. A little advance planning should allow any mountain lover to find a good spot to let his or her soul expand.

CHAPTER 5

Trips in Montana

GLACIER NATIONAL PARK

LIKE ALL NATIONAL Parks these days, Glacier has its crowded sections, filled with traffic jams and asphalt. Sections of the Park, however, seem to be free of overcrowding, and because the scenery here is so different from anywhere else in the U.S. Rockies, one of the less crowded parts of the Park has been included in this book.

Glacier is a land of big, steep mountains which have been glaciated quite recently and which are covered with dense forests on their lower slopes. Below are huge lakes filling the basins carved out by the now retreated glaciers and reflecting the mountains above. The mountains themselves are made up of conspicuous horizontal layers of sedimentary rock.

Cross-country travel in Glacier National Park is rather difficult because of steep slopes and dense vegetation, so most back-country travellers will stick to the trail system, at least below timberline. Water is rarely much of a problem.

The large and beautiful lakes in this country will have allure to anyone with a boat. Fortunately, motorboats are prohibited on most. Anyone taking a boat out on one of these lakes should be especially prudent since high winds and the resulting large waves can come up in an extremely short time, sweeping down from the mountain canyons above without warning.

It is wise to check on the availability of sites at the campground to which you are going as soon as you enter the Park. Day hiking is not controlled, but backpackers are required to obtain permits from a ranger before starting on the trail. Back-country campsites are regulated by the Park Service to prevent overuse and ecological damage.

Though bears are not a major problem in Glacier, there are both blacks and grizzlies present, so it is wise to take reasonable precautions. Don't leave food lying around at night, and *never* keep food in your tent. Try to avoid very strong-smelling foods, particularly in containers that will carry over for several meals. Thus, if you are carrying sardines on a backpacking trip, wash and burn out the can after use rather than having your camps smell of sardines for the next week. On backpacking trips, hang food out of reach and well away from the camp. Don't go to sleep in the middle of any trail, whether it is a maintained one or a game path. By thorough washing keep the remains and odor of any smelly foods off yourself and your equipment, particularly items you keep near you when you are sleeping. Avoid perfumed cosmetics and soap, which also attract bears. When hiking on trails where the visibility is poor, sing, whistle, talk, or use a noisemaker to warn bears of your approach. Like humans, bears are most dangerous when taken by surprise. Cubs, and this includes some pretty good sized yearlings, are never far from their mothers, and the last thing that any sane person wants to do is to come between the old sow and her children, so if you should see a small bear, go back the way you came. Don't try to get too close to any large wild animal or challenge its right to pass on a trail—a

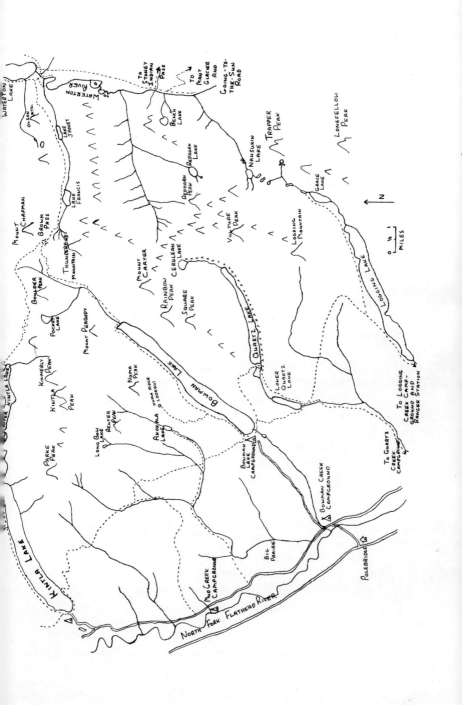

little respect without overt fear goes a long way towards preventing unpleasant experiences.

Approaches

The section of Glacier National Park recommended here is in its northwest corner. Those visiting other parts of the Park may come in from the Going-to-the-Sun Highway. Two parallel gravel roads lead towards this corner of the Park along opposite sides of the North Fork of the Flathead River. The North Fork Road is inside the Park and is reached by entering the Park through West Glacier, turning left on the Camas Creek Road after a couple of miles, and then, 1½ miles further on, turning right on the Fish Creek-North Fork Road. From this junction it is another 27 miles on the gravel road to the turnoff for Bowman Lake Campground and 42 miles to Kintla Lake.

The parallel road is across the river in the Flathead National Forest. It is actually the more scenic route, because the open space over the river permits a better look at the country rising over the Flathead. A bridge connects the two roads at Polebridge, just south of the turnoff for Bowman Lake. Before going up the Forest Service road, however, one should make inquiries to make sure the bridge is open. Gasoline is available at Polebridge, but not on the North Fork Road, so it is best to start with a full tank. The Polebridge Road can be reached by taking the Camas Creek Road described above or by going directly from the Town of Columbia Falls. It connects on the north with a dirt road going into British Columbia and connecting to Elko, Fernie, and Michel.

There are many ways of reaching the west side of the Park to make these connections, all clear enough from highway maps. The simplest are probably U.S. Route 2 from either the east or west and U.S. Route 93 coming from the south, where it connects with Interstate 90, 8 miles west of Missoula.

Campgrounds

The two campgrounds most recommended here are those at

the lower ends of Bowman Lake and Kintla Lake. Each has a view up one of Glacier's spectacular lakes to the peaks. The picture on the cover of this book was taken at Bowman Lake, perhaps the more spectacular of the two. Either is an excellent base for short walks, long backpacking trips, boating, or fishing. Bowman Lake has 48 campsites and Kintla 29. The distance to Kintla Lake has already been mentioned. Bowman Lake is 6 miles up the access road from the North Fork Road. Both campgrounds have piped water and pit toilets, and there is normally wood available, but it will need to be split. There are ranger stations at both campgrounds where you can obtain information, backcountry permits, and advice.

There are several other campgrounds in the area which connect with the trail system shown on the map. Bowman Creek Campground is near the turnoff for Bowman Lake and has 7 campsites, but water must be obtained from the creek. Mud Creek Campground, with 3 sites and a pump, is about halfway between Bowman Creek and Kintla Lake. Quartz Creek Campground is 6 miles south of Bowman Creek, has 5 sites and a pump. It is about 6 miles up the trail (which leaves the road just north of the campground) to Lower Quartz Lake, which is shown on the accompanying map. Eight miles south of Bowman Creek is Logging Creek Campground, near the ranger station of the same name. It has 10 sites, and water is obtained from the creek. The lower end of Logging Lake, shown on the map, is about 4½ miles up the trail that follows the creek.

Hikes

There are dozens of possible hikes from either Bowman Lake or Kintla Lake Campground, beginning with walks along the trails that follow the shores of the lakes. Such trails generally work up and down a good deal as they go through the stream courses feeding into the lakes, and panoramic views are occasional, rather than continuous, because of the densely wooded slopes leading down to the lake shores. The lakes themselves are so long that hiking the length of one of them and back may easily consume a day of moderate walking. There is no need for detailed mention of these hikes below, since one can simply start off at any time of day and go as long as one wants to.

FROM BOWMAN LAKE CAMPGROUND:

Head of Bowman Lake—14 miles; 1000 feet. The trail goes around the north side of the lake and is easy to find. There is a designated backcountry campsite at the head of the lake. Maps: Kintla Peak, 7½', Quartz Ridge, 7½', Mount Carter, 7½'.

Numa Ridge Lookout—10 miles; 2700 feet. Start off on the trail around the lake. The trail up to Numa Ridge, which rises on the north side of the lake, goes off to the left after about ¾ mile. Maps: Kintla Peak, 7½', Quartz Ridge, 7½'.

Akokala Lake—12 miles; 2000 feet. The trail to Akokala Lake begins on the north end of Bowman Lake Campground, near the ranger station and the start of the trail around the lake. It climbs over the ridge on the north side of Bowman Lake and then drops down to meet Akokala Creek after about 3½ miles. Here there is a trail junction, with a trail going down the creek to meet the North Fork Road, another continuing north from just down the creek to go to Kintla Lake, and the trail to Akokala Lake going up the valley. There is a backcountry campsite at Akokala Lake for those who want to make this a backpacking trip. Maps: Kintla Peak, 7½', Quartz Ridge, 7½'.

Lower Quartz Lake—8 miles; 2100 feet. The Quartz Lakes lie in the next glacial valley south of Bowman. The trail goes off from south of the campground, first crossing Bowman Creek on a large bridge and then climbing over the ridge to the south. There is a backcountry campsite at the foot of Lower Quartz Lake. Map: Quartz Ridge, 7½'.

Upper Quartz Lake—14 miles; 2600 feet. From Lower Quartz Lake, the trail continues on up the watershed past a little lake (Middle Quartz Lake) to the foot of the much larger Quartz Lake. Here there is another backcountry campsite. The high peak at the head of the lake is Vulture Peak. Map: Quartz Ridge, 7½'.

FROM KINTLA LAKE CAMPGROUND:

Backpacking Trips

Most of the hikes listed above will serve nicely for moderate two-day backpacking trips. Those who are more ambitious or who have more time should be able to find something to their tastes in the following list.

Grace Lake—32 miles; 5600 feet. Take the trail from Bowman Lake to Lower Quartz Lake. Thence, follow the trail to Logging Lake, and on reaching the trail somewhat above the lake turn left, going along the north side of Logging Lake for about 3 miles, then upstream for another 1½ miles to Grace Lake. There are backcountry campsites at the foot of Lower Quartz Lake, at the middle and the top of Logging Lake, and at both ends of Grace Lake. Maps: Quartz Ridge, 7½′, Demers Ridge, 7½′, Camas Ridge West, 7½′, Vulture Peak, 7½′, Mount Geduhn, 7½′.

Head of Kintla Lake—13 miles; 400 feet. The trail around the lake is on the north side. There is a backcountry campground at the upper end of the lake. Maps: Kintla Lake, 7½′, Kintla Peak, 7½′.

Upper Kintla Lake—18 miles; 800 feet. Continuing along the same trail for another 2½ miles brings the hiker to Upper Kintla Lake. It is still another 3½ miles to the upper end of the lake. There are backcountry campsites at both ends. Maps: Kintla Lake, 7½′, Kintla Peak, 7½′.

Kintla-Bowman-Waterton Lakes Circuit—66 miles; 10,400 feet (can be shortened in many ways). This trip can be started from either Kintla or Bowman, of course, but it is described here as leaving from Bowman. Take the trail around the north side of the lake. It is 7 miles to the backcountry campsite at the head of the lake. The trail then continues up the gentle, wooded valley of Bowman Creek for another 4½ miles before beginning to climb steeply up the cirque at its head towards Brown Pass

(6255 feet). At Brown Pass the trail to Kintla Lake comes in from the right, and those wishing a shorter trip can take it, eliminating the Waterton Lake section of the hike and reducing the length by 17 miles. The trail down to Waterton Lake follows the Olson Creek drainage, with fine views of Logan Falls and the Thunderbird Glacier on the descent. The first lake one comes to, a couple of miles beyond the pass, is Lake Francis. There are backcountry campsites a little above the lake and at its foot. Another 3 miles down is Lake Janet, and Waterton Lake (Goat Haunt) is 3½ past that. There are campsites and trail shelters at Waterton Lake, as well as a ranger station. The trail leading north along the west side of the lake goes to the headquarters of Waterton Lakes National Park in Canada, while trails leading south connect with other parts of Glacier. There are several fine short hikes to waterfalls near the foot of Waterton Lake. For the leg to Kintla Lake, the hiker first goes back up the valley to Brown Pass. Taking the right fork at Brown Pass, one continues to climb and follows a spectacular traverse around the cirque at the head of Bowman Valley. After about 1½ miles the hiker comes to a beautiful little cirque called Hole-in-the-Wall, where there is a backcountry campsite. There are two branches of the trail after one passes the bottom of the cirque, which meet higher up. The lower trail is easier and shorter, with less altitude gain, but the higher one is more spectacular. In either case, one climbs on up to Boulder Pass (7500 feet); on the other side there is a backcountry campsite. From here the trail drops down to the Kintla Lakes. It is about 5 miles down from Boulder Pass to the head of Upper Kintla Lake. The trail from here to the lower end of Kintla Lake has been discussed in the hikes section. There are backcountry campsites at both ends of Upper Kintla Lake and at the Upper end of Kintla. From the automobile campground at the lower end of Kintla Lake, the trail to Bowman Lake starts by going around the foot of the lake and starting along the south shore. It then climbs Parke Ridge and meets the trail from Bowman to Akokala Lake (see hike above) after crossing several streams. The distance from Kintla to Bowman by this trail is 12 miles, with a 2400 foot altitude gain. Maps: Kintla Lake, 7½′, Kintla Peak, 7½′,

Quartz Ridge, 7½', Polebridge, 7½', Mount Carter, 7½', Porcupine Ridge, 7½'.

BITTERROOTS

The Bitterroots form an extensive chain of mountains several hundred miles long. The crest of this range makes up most of the border between Montana and Idaho, and the southern portion is the Continental Divide after it swings west from the Bob Marshall Wilderness. The Bitterroot country is mostly beautiful, forested land, dissected here and there by great river canyons. Here and there jagged peaks rise above timberline, but the peaks are not exceptionally high, and the surrounding region lies at elevations of around 4000 feet.

The Bitterroot Range is the watershed for some of the finest wild rivers remaining in North America, including the Salmon and the Selway, and some ambitious backpackers may want to consider trips into the river gorges. Round trips into some spots along the Middle Fork of the Salmon require over 100 miles of hiking.

The section chosen for inclusion here is at the edge of the Selway-Bitterroot Wilderness, which lies along the border of Idaho and Montana, but is not on the Continental Divide. The section shown on the accompanying map is high enough so that some of the trails go above timberline, giving hikers a good view of the surrounding country. The Blodgett Canyon is an impressive introduction to the gorges of the region, though it was cut by a fairly small creek.

The Montana side of the crest is in Bitterroot National Forest, and the Idaho side is in Clearwater National Forest. One of the approaches from the Idaho side is discussed in that state's section.

This is generally a good region to visit early in the year, because it is low enough so that the snow is fairly well melted out early. Muddy roads and stream crossings can present a real problem, however.

Approaches

Hamilton and Victor, which are shown on the accompanying map, are located on U.S. Route 93, south of Missoula, Montana. Missoula is on Interstate 90. From southern Idaho, 93 goes north from Twin Falls, which is located on Interstate 80N. Victor is 35 miles south of Missoula.

Access roads to the various trailheads are shown on the accompanying map, but not all the roads in the area are shown. These can be confusing, and it is best to get local directions.

Campgrounds

There are few Forest Service campgrounds on the Montana side of the Wilderness Area, though there are commercially operated campgrounds along U.S. 93. Those using other trailheads than Blodgett Creek will usually be able to find adequate campsites on Forest Service land along the creeks, but out of courtesy and prudence, one should not camp on private land along approach roads without permission of property owners.

The spot on Blodgett Creek is a good spot to camp in a spectacular canyon, but its facilities are primitive. There are larger campgrounds on the Lake Como Road, which goes west almost to the crest a few miles south of Hamilton. The canyons in the area shown are far less developed, however, and Blodgett Canyon provides a satisfactory location for car camping, while backpackers will find that walking a little way up any of the creeks will bring them to fine spots.

Hikes

There are good short hikes up any of the canyons going westward towards the Bitterroots, and there is little point in listing them. Close to the crest there are generally several small lakes nestled up against the slopes and cliffs of the peaks. A couple of

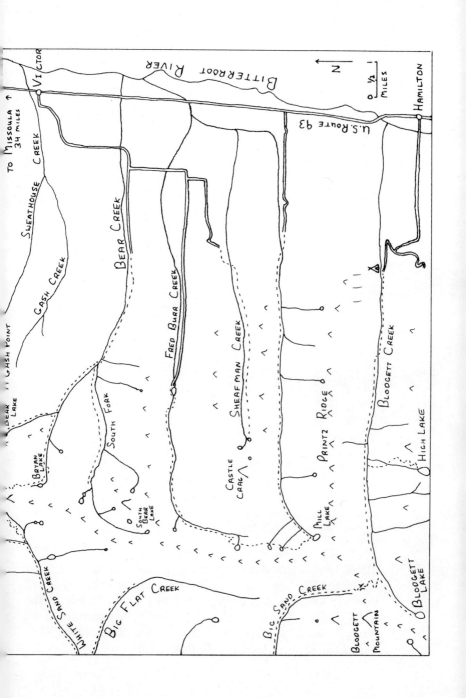

these are listed below, but there is hardly a need for route description in this area. The canyons are all roughly parallel, running east from the peaks to the Bitterroot River along Route 93.

Blodgett Canyon to High Lake—18 miles; 3200 feet. From the roadhead and campsite in Blodgett Canyon west of Hamilton, take the trail up Blodgett Creek for about 6 miles. Here a creek and a side trail climb steeply south to High Lake, a lovely spot with a fine view. Return the same way. Maps: Hamilton, North, 7½′, Printz Ridge, 7½′.

South Fork Bear Creek—16 miles; 2000 feet. From the Bear Creek roadhead southwest of Victor (be sure to get local directions) take the trail west to Bear Creek. The trail and the creek fork 3½ miles upstream. Here the Middle and North Forks go northwest, while the South Fork continues west. Continue upstream for another 4½ miles for excellent views of the crest. Return the same way. Maps: Victor, 7½′; Gash Point, 7½′; White Sand Lake, 7½′.

Backpacking Trips

Either of the hikes just described would make good short backpacking jaunts, as would trips up any of the canyons in the area. Backpacks over to the Idaho side can be long and interesting. Three trips of moderate length are described below.

Blodgett Lake—24 miles; 2500 feet. From the roadhead and campsite in Blodgett Canyon, take the trail upstream, following the creek all the way to its head at Blodgett Lake, just below the crest of the range. Return the same way. Maps: Hamilton, North, 7½′; Printz Ridge, 7½′; Blodgett Mountain, 7½′.

Big Sand Creek—26 miles; 3500 feet. Ten miles up Blodgett Creek from the roadhead, as the creek begins to turn south, the trail up to Blodgett Pass branches off to the right. Take this trail up over the pass, and drop down into the wide valley of Big Sand Creek on the Idaho side. There are good campsites in the valley. Return the same way. Maps: Hamilton, North, 7½′; Printz Ridge, 7½′; Blodgett Mountain, 7½′.

South Bear Lake—22 miles; 3500 feet. This route is likely to involve a little bushwhacking, but the scenery and the solitude are worth it. Take the route described for the hike up the South Fork of Bear Creek. Continue following poor trails along the main creek as it turns southward, climbing steadily. The head of the creek is South Bear Lake, tucked up in a little cirque among the peaks. A fine place. Return the same way. Maps: Victor, 7½ '; Gash Point, 7½ '; White Sand Lake, 7½ '; Blodgett Mountain, 7½ '.

BOB MARSHALL WILDERNESS

The Bob Marshall Wilderness is certainly one of the finest roadless areas still left in the United States, south of Alaska. Its area is nearly a million acres, extending along the Continental Divide a little south of Glacier National Park. In combination with the Scapegoat Wilderness, which adjoins it to the south (and which will henceforth be considered along with Bob Marshall), it includes over half the length of the Divide within the State of Montana.

This is an area for real wilderness lovers who want to travel far into the backcountry. There is no easy road access to alpine regions in this area—the only way to really become familiar with the country is to walk or ride a horse. Huge forested tracts with thousands of miles of rivers and streams surround the peaks. Though there are fine short hikes into the wilderness from automobile campgrounds, one cannot really penetrate to the heart of the Bob Marshall Wilderness on day hikes. It is easy to plan backpacking circuits of well over 100 miles here without even having to backtrack.

There are fine examples of high glaciated cliffs in the Bob Marshall Wilderness, with the 15-mile-long Chinese Wall, a cliff of 1000 feet, being an excellent example. Still, this is generally a rather gentle wilderness, with hills that are rolling and wooded. It

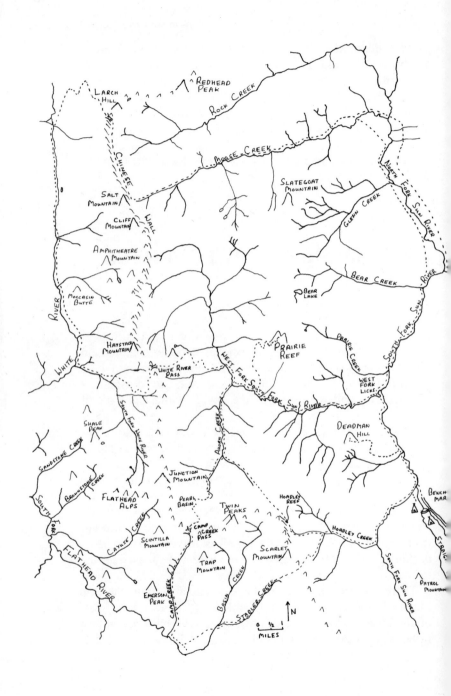

is good country for long family backpacks. There is a lot of wildlife, and the fishing is superb.

Approaches

Though there are a number of ways into the Bob Marshall Wilderness, the trails described here all leave from Benchmark Campground. Drive to Augusta, Montana on U.S. Route 287. There is a ranger station in Augusta, where one can get information or directions if needed. The road to Benchmark and Wood Lake goes west from Augusta (not from 287 south of Augusta as indicated on a number of maps) 14 miles on a county road and then 16 miles southwest on Forest Service Road 235.

Campsites

At Benchmark there are actually two campsites a short distance from one another, which between them have a total of 17 campsites with water. There is also the Wood Lake Campground, 6 miles further back on the road, with 7 campsites.

Hikes

Deadman Hill—9 miles; 2100 feet. Take the trail going north along the west bank of the South Fork Sun River. The trail to the top of Deadman Hill branches off to the left after about 2 miles. Maps: Benchmark, 7½', and Pretty Prairie, 7½'.

Continental Divide via Hoadley Creek—17 miles; 1800 feet. From Benchmark cross over the South Fork Sun River to the west side. The trail up Hoadley Creek turns off after about 3½ miles, heading off to the right. A couple of miles farther on the trail forks, with the left fork going up to the Divide just south of Scarlet Mountain. Maps: Benchmark, 7½', and Trap Mountain, 7½'.

Other Hikes—Trails in all directions from Benchmark follow the Sun River and its tributary streams, and going along them for any distance will make a pleasant hike. As we noted earlier, however, getting into the heart of this wilderness requires a long trek, too long to be covered in a day by the average hiker. (This is appropriate in a special way since Bob Marshall, the great conservationist for whom the region was named, was a phenomenal hiker, often covering distances of 50 miles in a day.)

Backpacking Trips

Prairie Reef— 26 miles; 4000 feet. The hike to Prairie Reef makes a nice two-day backpack with a good view from the top of much of the eastern part of the Bob Marshall Wilderness, including the Chinese Wall, a great limestone cliff which runs along the Continental Divide to the northwest. Take the trail north along the South Fork of the Sun River 4½ miles to West Fork Licks. Here the West Fork South Fork Sun River (yes, that's what it's called) comes in from the left, and the route follows the trail on its north side. The trail up Prairie Reef goes off to the right about 5½ miles farther on. Maps: Benchmark, 7½'; Pretty Prairie, 7½'; Prairie Reef, 7½'.

Danaher Basin-Pearl Basin Circuit—40 miles; 6000 feet. This fine hike will allow the visitor a real taste of the country. The difficulty of the trails is quite modest, so it is a walk well suited to families, providing they allow enough time. Strong backpackers could make the circuit in two days, while a leisurely trip could take the better part of a week. Begin by following the trail described for the Continental Divide via Hoadley Creek. Cross the Divide and follow the trail on down Stadler Creek to the Basin on Danaher Creek. A few miles further down this creek empties into the South Fork of the Flathead River, a walk which makes a pleasant side trip in the afternoon. The Basin itself was the site of homesteading in the late 19th century. The route goes northwest along the Basin for a mile or so to the confluence with Camp Creek, which comes in from the right. Follow the trail up Camp Creek until the Divide is again reached at Camp Creek Pass, perhaps 6 miles up. The trail now drops into beautiful Pearl Basin and then follows the drainage of Ahorn Creek down to the West Fork South Fork

Sun River. Following the trail along the river downstream brings the hiker to West Fork Licks at the confluence with the South Fork, where the route turns up the South Fork to return to Benchmark. Maps: Benchmark, 7½'; Trap Mountain, 7½'; Prairie Reef, 7½'.

Chinese Wall—White River Circuit—65 miles; 6400 feet. Take the route described for Prairie Reef, down the South Fork of the Sun and then up the West Fork South Fork. Continue past the trails going right to Prairie Reef and left up Ahorn Creek. About a mile beyond the trail up Ahorn Creek to Camp Creek Pass, take the trail going left up Indian Creek to White River Pass. Three miles down from the pass is the South Fork of the White River, which the trail follows for another 2 miles to its confluence with the main stream of the White. The route then follows the White upstream for 10 miles, past lovely Needle Falls and many peaks, before turning uphill to cross the Divide at Larch Hill Pass. This brings the hiker to the north end of the Chinese Wall, and the trail now heads south below the Wall for 3 miles. The Wall continues with no trail following it, and cross-country hikers may want to scramble along it, but the trail turns down Burnt Creek, after passing an earlier turnoff at Moose Creek. Burnt Creek runs into the West Fork South Fork of the Sun, which the route follows to the South Fork. Following the South Fork upstream brings the hiker back to Benchmark. Maps: Benchmark, 7½'; Pretty Prairie, 7½'; Prairie Reef, 7½'; Haystack Mountain, 7½'; Amphitheatre Mountain, 7½'; Slategoat Mountain, 7½'.

CHAPTER 6

Trips in Idaho

BITTERROOTS

AN INTRODUCTION TO the Bitterroots has already been made in the section on the Montana side. On the Idaho side, approaches tend to be longer, and the terrain is more gentle, except for the deeper canyons. The accompanying map shows the general approaches and trails along the Idaho side of the crest adjoining the area covered under Montana. Long trips can be planned combining the two, especially if a car shuttle is planned.

There is a ranger station at Powell, and information can be obtained there. The roads to Elk Summit and Colt Creek may vary, and their condition should be checked before driving in.

Approaches

Powell is on U.S. Route 12, 70 miles north of Lowell, Idaho, and 45 miles south of Lolo, Montana, and the junction with U.S. 95, 56 miles southwest of Missoula on Interstate 90. From Lolo one drives over Lolo Pass, on the Idaho-Montana border, and proceeds another 12 miles to Powell.

Campgrounds

There is a good campground with 34 sites at Powell, as well as several other campgrounds along Route 12. Check on the situation of the roadhead campgrounds at the ranger station at Powell, before driving in. Either Colt Creek or Elk Summit makes a good base for hiking or backpacking trips.

Hikes

As on the eastern side of the Bitterroot crest, there are good walks along any of the creeks, but their courses are far more chaotic in Idaho, and the distance to the main peaks is farther. From Colt Creek, one can hike upstream for short or long distances. From Elk Summit, there is first a climb across a saddle and then a drop to Big Sand Creek. Some longer hikes follow.

Elk Summit-Big Sand Lake—15 miles; 1300 feet. Take the trail which climbs a low rise west of Elk Summit and drops down to Big Sand Creek. Follow the trail up the creek to Big Sand Lake. Return the same way. Map: Jeanette Mountain, 7½'.

Colt Creek-White Sand Creek—16 miles; 1500 feet. Take the trail going up the main river below Colt Creek, and stay on the north side at the next two large forks. This brings the hiker into the fine, gentle valley of White Sand Creek. The trail leads on up to the pass over the crest to the Middle Fork of Bear Creek, shown in the Montana Bitterroot section. Return the same way. Maps: Savage Ridge, 7½'; White Sand Lake, 7½'.

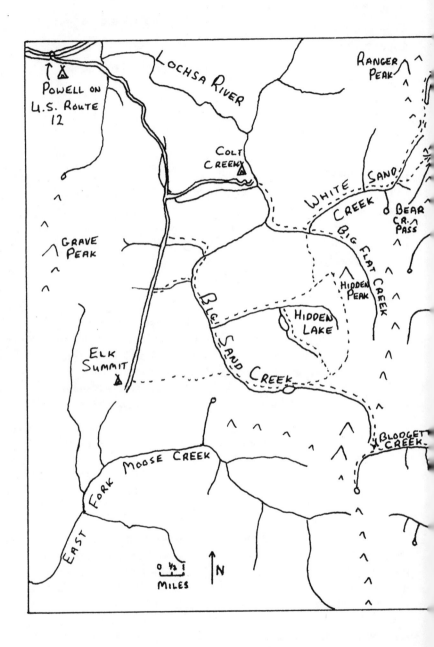

Backpacking Trips

There are many possible backpacking trips in the area, some of which should be suggested by the map. Very long trips can be taken into the region south of the one shown. The suggested trip below is of moderate length and goes over to the Montana side of the crest.

Colt Creek-Bear Creek Pass-Bryan Lake—24 miles; 3500 feet. Take the trail up White Sand Creek, as described above. Fifteen miles from the Colt Creek Campground and 5½ miles above the junction with Big Sand Creek, the trail forks. The southern fork goes up to Bear Creek Pass, and the trail on the other side drops down to Bryan Lake, which is shown on the Montana Bitterroots map. Return the same way. Maps: Savage Ridge, 7½'; White Sand Lake, 7½'.

SAWTOOTH MOUNTAINS

The Sawtooth Range is not exceptionally high, with the larger peaks rising to elevations between 10,500 and 11,000 feet, but it has long been a favorite area among connoisseurs of rugged mountain wilderness. The Sawtooths are spectacular and exceptionally beautiful. There are hundreds of jagged peaks and spires rising above perhaps two hundred delightful lakes. This is the kind of range that most mountain lovers visualize when dreaming of the peaks.

The Sawtooth Range varies a good deal in accessibility. The eastern part of the region is perhaps a little too easy to reach. Redfish Lake, a lovely long body of water which reflects a couple of dozen surrounding summits, is only a couple of miles drive off U.S. Route 93, so that it is often rather crowded during the height of the season. On the other hand, the drive to the southwestern approaches is longer and less well-known, and it is this approach which is recommended in this book. From this direction, the visitor is unlikely to be troubled by excessive numbers of fellow countrymen.

The Sawtooth area can be equally pleasant for car campers who want to do a little hiking or fishing, ardent backpackers, or mountaineers. Day hikes will bring walkers up to the bases of the outer peaks. The trail system is very well-maintained and marked, so that multi-day trips are not difficult to manage, even for novices. The country is very hilly, though, so a lot of up and down should be anticipated. Don't expect to cover great distances in a day unless you are exceptionally strong.

Cross-country hikers and climbers will also find plenty to challenge them—each side canyon coming down to a trail holds the promise of blue lakes surrounded by cliffs and spires above. Fishermen will also find plenty to keep them happy.

Approaches

The recommended starting point for Sawtooth trips is the tiny town of Atlanta. The easiest way to get there is from the west, taking Idaho State Route 21 southeast from Boise for 13 miles. Here, Route 25 turns north, away from Lucky Peak Reservoir, and a gravel road continues west along the shore of the reservoir. It is not quite 50 miles up the Middle Fork of the Boise River to Atlanta. Atlanta can also be reached from State Route 68 to the south; 68 runs between Mountain Home on Interstate 80N to U.S. 93 just south of Bellevue. A gravel road leaves 68 at Dixie and runs through Pine and Featherville. This route is used if one is approaching on 68 from the west. If one is coming from the east on 68, a gravel road turns off for Featherville at Fairfield. From Featherville it is another 16 miles north at Atlanta. Whichever of these approaches is used, it is well to fill the gas tank just before leaving the main highway.

Campgrounds

There are a number of campgrounds on the roads into Atlanta. The best one for approaches to the Sawtooths is the Power Plant Campground, operated by Boise National Forest.

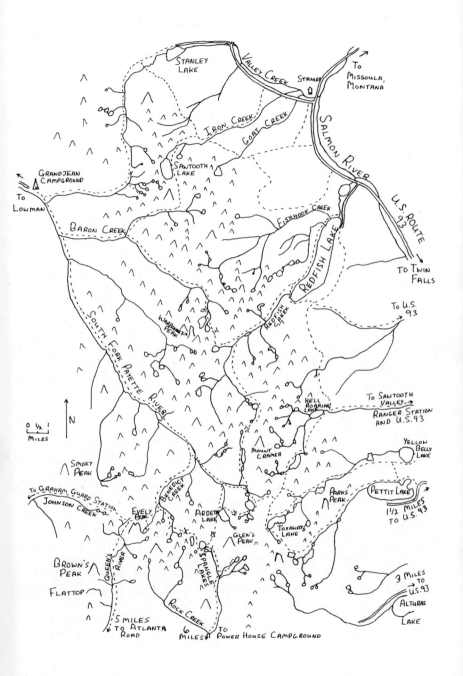

It is a couple of miles east of Atlanta and has 24 campsites. Trails lead directly from this campground into the Sawtooth Primitive Area.

More information can be obtained at the Forest Supervisor's Headquarters in Boise, at the Dutch Creek Ranger Station, about 10 miles west of Atlanta on the road coming in from State Route 21, and sometimes at the Atlanta Guard Station.

Hikes

The main trail into the Sawtooths goes upstream from the Power House Campground, and pleasant short hikes can be taken any distance up this trail for views of the high country beyond. One can also walk or drive a few miles west from Atlanta to the confluence of the Queen's River with the Boise. Here, another trail goes north into the primitive area. The hikes listed below follow these two trails, and shortened versions of them will be found to be quite pleasant for those who are less ambitious.

Spangle Lakes—20 miles; 3200 feet. Take the trail upstream (northeast) from the Power House Campground. About 4 miles up, a trail branches off to the right up Mattingly Creek to Alturas Lake. Continue up the left-hand fork. After another 4 miles another right-hand branch goes up to Camp Lake. The Spangle Lakes are about 2 miles past this junction, along the left fork. There are peaks all around and still more lakes beyond. Return the same way. Maps: A & B (see accompanying map).

Camp Lake—18 miles; 3200 feet. Take the same trail as that for the Spangle Lakes, but take the right fork after about 8 miles. Return the same way. Maps: A&B. (Note: Maps A through D are U.S.G.S. maps.)

Evely Peak—18 miles; 3000 feet. Take the trail up the Queen's River described above. An access road which may be in poor condition goes up the river to the trailhead. From the Boise River it is about 6 miles until one passes a mountain called Flattop, rising on the left. The river and the trail then climb more steeply towards Evely Peak, which the trail passes on the left. Return the same way. Maps: A, B, & C. (See heading *Maps,* following.)

Backpacking Trips

Any of the hikes listed above will make fine two- or three-day backpacking trips for many hikers. A trail circles most of the way around Evely (keeping the mountain to the right) and reaches a good lake for camping. The other hikes end at fine lakes. Two moderate circuits are listed below, and others of longer duration are obvious from the map.

Spangle Lakes-Queen's River Circuit—31 (or 24) miles; 4500 feet. This circuit takes the Spangle Lakes Trail, continues west along that trail past Ingeborg Lake, climbs a few hundred feet over a pass to the Benedict Creek drainage, follows that creek down for 1½ miles to the confluence with the creek coming down from Mount Evely, and takes the trail up that creek, around the north side of Evely and down the Queen's River. The trailhead at the Queen's River is described in the hikes section, If a car is left there, one can drive back past Atlanta to the Power House Campground, making a 24-mile hiking circuit. If this stretch is walked, an extra 7 miles is added. Maps: A, B, & C.

Spangle Lakes-Ardeth Lake-Queen's River Circuit— 36 (or 29) miles; 6000 feet. Take the trail to Spangle Lakes and then follow the trail northeast over a pass to Ardeth Lake. Follow the trail downstream for about 3 miles to the confluence with Benedict Creek, near some nice rapids and waterfalls. Turn south up Benedict Creek, turning right at the fork 3 miles up, and finishing as with the preceding circuit. Maps: A, B, C, & D.

Maps

At the time of this writing, mapping of the Sawtooth Region by the Geological Survey is not yet complete. Forest Service maps are available, and can be picked up at the Headquarters or

Ranger Station listed above, but no contours are shown. U.S.G.S. maps can be purchased for the east side of the range, which is shown on the accompanying map, but is not included in the hikes listed. For the area covered here, there are advance sheets available which include contours, but not all other information. They are 7½' sheets, cost 75c each, and can be ordered by giving coordinates from the Western Mapping Center, U.S.G.S., 345 Middlefield Road, Menlo Park, California 94025. The coordinates for the quadrangles covered here are: A: 115° 00' to 115° 7½' west longitude; 43° 45' to 43° 52½' north latitude; B: 115° 00' to 115° 7½' west longitude; 43° 52½' to 44° 00' north latitude; C: 115° 7½' to 115° 15' west longitude; 43° 45' to 43° 52½' north latitude; D: 115° 7½' to 115° 15' west longitude; 43° 52½' to 44° 00' north latitude. The completed maps should be available from normal U.S.G.S. sources within a couple of years.

CHAPTER 7

Trips in Wyoming

GROS VENTRE RANGE

THE GROSS VENTRE Range is relatively small, compared to the Wind Rivers or the Big Horns, but it is a fine and rugged region, full of deep, forested canyons and fine peaks of sedimentary rock. The range runs southeastward from Jackson Hole, and it is much less well-known than the neighboring Tetons. Despite its proximity to Grand Teton and Yellowstone National Parks, the Gros Ventre Range is not heavily used or much visited except during hunting season (beginning in the second week of September), when it should be avoided by family campers and most backpackers.

There is a fine pool, fed by a hot spring and maintained by the Forest Service, just up the trail from the campground recom-

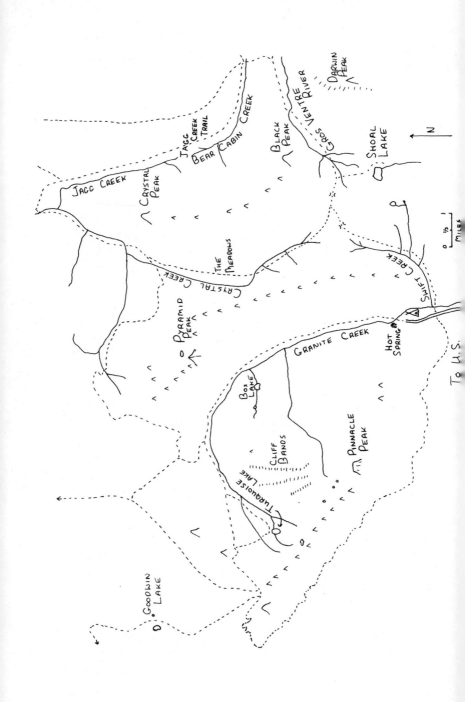

mended here, where one can go swimming for a nominal fee. A good soaking is welcome after a long day on the trail or the road, and it will add to the attractiveness of this fine area.

The hiking in the Gros Ventre Range is very pleasant, whether one is looking for a moderate stroll or a fairly rugged trip, and cross-country travel here will provide a challenging experience for the experienced wilderness lover looking for solitude in the high country. The fishing is quite good in most of the streams and lakes.

Approaches

There are a number of ways to come into the Gros Ventres, but the campground recommended here is approached from the south, on a road coming in from U.S. Route 187-189. Driving south from Jackson, one will come to the 187-189 turnoff in 13 miles, and the Granite Creek Road goes off to the north after another 12 miles. From Interstate 80, take 187 north from Rock Springs if travelling from the east or 189 north just beyond Evanston if coming from the west. The Granite Creek Road goes off a little over 150 miles from the interstate on 187 and about 185 miles on 189.

Campground

The Granite Creek Campground, with 72 campsites, is located 8½ miles up the Granite Creek Road, near Granite Falls and about a mile from the hot springs mentioned above. The hikes listed below all leave from the area of this pleasant campground.

Hikes

Three trails leave from the area of Granite Creek Campground, and each of them can be used either for short hikes or to connect with other trails for long backpacking circuits. In addition to the longer hikes and backpacks described in detail, hikes of any length along these trails are very pleasant.

Family camping in the Rockies has many lighthearted moments; a bath is nice after a day on the trail.

The easiest is the Granite Creek Trail, which continues up the creek beyond the hot springs. It has a gentle gradient and is good for family hikes of any distance.

Granite Creek Trail to Base of Pyramid Peak—12 miles; 1100 feet. Follow the trail up Granite Creek past the hot springs. The trail proceeds north towards Pyramid Peak for about 6 miles past the campground, before swinging to the left. The hike is up a deep, forested valley. Maps: Granite Falls, 7½', Crystal Peak, 7½'.

Base of Pinnacle Peak—17 miles; 2700 feet. From below the campground, a trail climbs the ridge to the west and then countours around to the drainage of Little Granite Creek, continuing then along the side of the range at the same altitude for miles, before swinging around the end to meet other trails coming in from the north. Take this trail past the junction with the trail coming up from Little Granite Creek for a spectacular view of towering Pinnacle Peak. Maps: Granite Falls, 7½', Bull Creek, 7½', Turquoise Lake, 7½'.

Shoal Lake—14 miles; 5000 feet. This rugged hike follows the Swift Creek Trail up the creek from its confluence with Granite Creek, below the campground. The route goes over the pass at the head of the creek and then contours east around the hillside to meet the Crystal Creek Trail as it climbs east to the pass between Crystal Creek and the Gros Ventre River. The trail drops over the pass, and soon after, the branch climbing south leaves the trail going down the Gros Ventre. This trail to the right climbs over a ridge and drops down to Shoal Lake. Return by the same route. Maps: Granite Falls, 7½', Crystal Peak, 7½', Darwin Peak, 7½'.

Backpacking Trips

The Shoal Lake trip listed above makes a good backpacking trip, but not for beginners, because of the tough climbing. Several other routes are listed below.

Turquoise Lake—24 miles; 2500 feet. This fine backpacking

trip involves easy hiking, and it is a good trip for beginners and families with children, and there is good fishing all along the way. It makes a good two-day trip for stronger backpackers and a nice three- or four-day one for those who want a moderate pace. Follow the trail up Granite Creek, following it around as it swings west and then south to the lake. Return by the same route. Maps: Granite Falls, 7½′, Crystal Peak, 7½′, Turquoise Lake, 7½′.

Turquoise Lake Circuit—31 miles; 4500 feet. To make the Turquoise Lake trip more interesting and challenging, it can be turned into a circuit of the Pinnacle Peak section of the Gros Ventre Range. Take the route described above to the lake. A continuation of the Granite Creek Trail goes west without swinging south to the lake. This trail can be followed from the original junction or picked up more easily by following a trail that goes north and slightly west from the lake. In any case, follow this trail on its zig-zagging way to the west until it swings around the end of the mountains and heads southeast, past the south slopes of Pinnacle Peak, over the head of Little Granite Creek, and finally down to the Granite Creek Road just below the campground. Maps: Granite Falls, 7½′, Crystal Peak, 7½′, Turquoise Lake, 7½′, Bull Creek, 7½′.

Swift Creek-Jagg Creek-Crystal Creek Circuit—50 miles; 8000 feet. This fine and rugged trip makes a complete trip around the Crystal Peak-Black Peak section of the range. Begin by following the trail description for Shoal Lake, but after crossing the pass into the Gros Ventre River drainage, continue down the trail which follows the upper Gros Ventre River for about 7 miles to a trail swinging off to the left and going up Bear Cabin Creek. This trail finally climbs over a pass and follows Jagg Creek down past Crystal Peak to its confluence with Crystal Creek. Follow the trail going up Crystal Creek back up to the junction with the Swift Creek Trail and drop back down this to the campground. Maps: Granite Falls, 7½′, Crystal Peak, 7½′, Darwin Peak, 7½′, Upper Slide Lake, 7½′, Grizzly Lake, 7½′.

Those looking for even longer circuits can easily pick them

out on the accompanying map. From Crystal Creek, one can continue around to the north of Pyramid Peak and then return down Granite Creek or go on around past Turquoise Lake and south of Pinnacle Peak, as in the Turquoise Lake Circuit.

BIG HORNS

The Big Horn Mountains form a fine rugged range, not unlike the Wind Rivers to the west, but not nearly so well-known. The range presents many opportunities for hikers, backpackers, climbers, and fishermen. Access to the central part of the area can only be gained by backpackers, horsemen, or extremely hardy hikers, however, since the crest is set well back from the nearest roads. The Big Horns are wilderness mountains.

For precipitous cirques and mountain walls, the Big Horns are matched in Wyoming only by the Wind Rivers and the Tetons. The range is also strewn with lakes, which provide superb scenery, campsites, and fishing.

Trail-walking, cross-country travel, and mountaineering are all superb in the Big Horns, but only a few of the trails are signed, so a reasonable ability at reading maps is requisite on all but the most popular routes. The range receives only moderate precipitation, so that forests are not particularly dense, making for fairly easy cross-country travel, where the terrain is not too steep.

Approaches

The Big Horns can be approached from several directions, but the way recommended here comes in from the south, near where U.S. Route 16 crosses the range at Powder River Pass. Take 16 west from Buffalo, where Interstates 25 and 90 intersect. Cross the pass and continue until the road up West Tensleep Creek turns off to the north, about 50 miles from Buffalo. One can also pick up Route 16 from the west; it runs together with Routes 14 and 20 out of Yellowstone National Park and through Cody, turning south at Greybull and east again at Worland. From Lander take Wyoming 789 to Riverton, U.S. 26 to Shoshoni, U.S. 20 to Worland, where 16 is met. For drivers coming from the west, the turnoff is 20 miles past the town of Tensleep.

Campgrounds

There are a number of Forest Service campgrounds along Route 16 and on the West Tensleep Creek Road (signs to Tyrrell Ranger Station). Boulder Park, with 34 sites is on the other side of 16 from the approach road. Four miles north on the road, and 2 miles past Tyrrell Ranger Station, is Island Park Campground, with 10 campsites. Another 3½ miles north is the best camping place, and the one from which the trails listed here leave, West Tensleep Lake Campground, with 10 more campsites.

Hikes

Lost Twin Lakes—10½ miles; 1500 feet. This pleasant hike follows a trail northeast from West Tensleep Lake, following a drainage system that comes into West Tensleep Creek a little below the lake. A couple of miles up, the trail swings west, passing south of Mirror Lake, and continues up to the Lost Twin Lakes. Return the same way. Map: Lake Helen, 7½'.

Lake Helen—8 miles; 1000 feet. The main trail out of West Tensleep Lake Campground continues up West Tensleep Creek. Lake Helen is an easy 4 miles north. Map: Lake Helen, 7½'.

Marion Lake—10 miles; 1100 feet. Follow the West Tensleep Creek Trail another mile past Lake Helen. Map: Lake Helen, 7½'.

Mistymoon Lake—12 miles; 1300 feet. Continue past Marion Lake for another mile. Map: Lake Helen, 7½'.

Medicine Cabin Park—21 miles; 3400 feet. This hike crosses

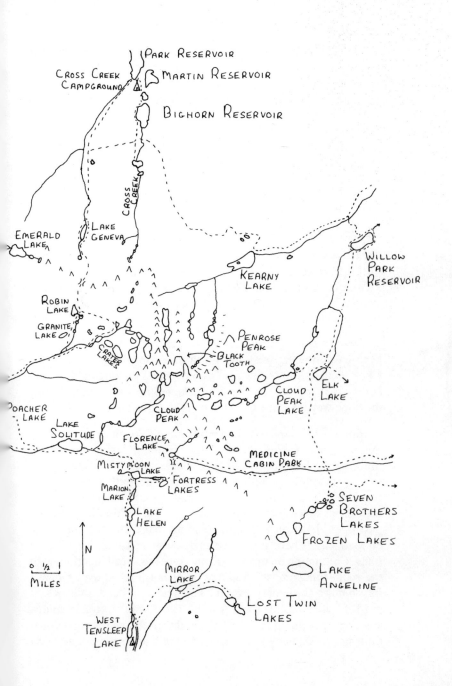

the Divide and passes some spectacular alpine country. Hike to Mistymoon Lake and take the trail which heads west around the south side of the lake. Pass the Fortress Lakes, climb up to Florence Pass, and drop down to Florence Lake on the other side. The trail down the creek that drains Florence brings the hiker to Medicine Cabin Park (which makes a good campsite) after another 3 miles. Those wanting some interesting cross-country exploring may want to investigate the small lakes above Florence to the northeast. Return the same way. Maps: Lake Helen, 7½′, Lake Angeline, 7½′.

Backpacking Trips

Mistymoon Lake, Lost Twin Lakes, and Medicine Cabin Park all make good short backpacking goals, as does Solitude Lake, described below. For trips of intermediate length, a portion of the range circuit can be done, with as many side trips as time and energy permit.

Solitude Lake—22 miles; 2700 feet. From Mistymoon Lake keep left, climbing west and north to a rise with a fine view of Cloud Peak to the northeast. Drop down on the other side of the rise to Lake Solitude, a beautiful lake fed by a waterfall. Return the same way. Maps: Lake Helen, 7½′, Lake Solitude, 7½′.

Range Circuit—75 miles; 9100 feet. Take the trail to Lake Solitude, and follow the Solitude Trail on down the stream draining the lake for a couple of miles, until the Solitude Trail turns right uphill to climb over a divide to the north, branching off from the Rock Creek Trail. The trail passes Poacher Lake and then drops down into another drainage and follows it upstream, passing the junction with a trail coming up the stream from another roadhead. There is a large meadow here called Tepee Pole Flats. Continuing on upstream, one comes to a trail junction, with the route following the Solitude Trail north to go over Geneva Pass 4 miles away, past several lakes. The right-hand trail goes up to Cliff Lake; the cliff for which it is named can be seen from this area. One can go up to Cliff Lake and then follow poorly defined trails northwest back to the Solitude Trail, adding about an extra

3 miles to the route. Continue north from Geneva Pass past Lake Geneva. Five miles past the head of Lake Geneva, the Solitude Trail branches off to the right, while the trail down the creek continues towards Park Reservoir. Continue following the Solitude Trail over Cross Creek, around the head of the East Fork of Little Goose Creek, past Kearny Lake, down Kearny Creek, around Willow Park Reservoir, past Elk Lake, and then west at Medicine Cabin Park, just before reaching the Seven Brothers Lakes. The Solitude Trail then climbs up to Florence Lake and Florence Pass and drops down to Mistymoon Lake, from which the trail down West Tensleep Creek leads back to camp. The Solitude Trail is well marked throughout its length, and is easy enough to follow, but do not expect the same conditions on the numerous interesting side trips. Maps: Lake Helen, 7½', Lake Solitude, 7½', Shell Lake, 7½', Cloud Peak, 7½', Park Reservoir, 7½', Willow Park Reservoir, 7½', Lake Angeline, 7½'.

THE WIND RIVERS

The largest range of mountains in Wyoming is the Wind River Range, considered by many to be the finest stretch of mountains between the Canadian Border and South America. The Wind Rivers include active glaciers of fair size, peaks and spires with polished vertical walls carved and smoothed by grinding ice, all set in beautiful alpine country dotted with lakes. The fishing is good, the wild flowers beautiful, and many of the peaks are among the most spectacular in the country.

Though the Wind Rivers can be seen from the distance along a number of the state's highways, one cannot approach to intimate proximity without hiking a number of miles. This is one of the regions listed in the book which can only be admired from afar by car campers—backpacking is the best way to really become familiar with the Wind Rivers.

The Wind Rivers form the Continental Divide between the

Yellowstone-Teton region and the Great Basin to the south. The range is about 75 miles long, with many bends and offshoots, so that it forms a very large mountainous area, one which cannot be explored in one short visit. It includes parts of Bridger and Shoshone National Forests and of the Wind River Indian Reservation.

It is difficult to choose an area of the Wind Rivers to recommend to visitors, but the one shown here includes some of the most spectacular scenery in the Range, if not the highest peaks, and fine backpacking trips can be made without requiring mountaineering skills. Most of the area shown on the accompanying map is in the Popo Agie Wilderness, administered by Shoshone National Forest. Overnight trips into the backcountry require permits, which can be obtained at a ranger station. The number of permits for stays in popular areas may be limited to prevent overuse.

Approaches

There are trails into the Wind Rivers from both east and west. The region shown here is on the east side of the Continental Divide. The road shown on the map is reached from U.S. Route 287, between Rawlins on Interstate 80 and Yellowstone National Park. The access road (to Dickinson Park and Mosquito Park) leaves 287 15 miles north of Lander and a mile south of Fort Washakie. It may also be reached by taking U.S. 26 west from Casper and turning south to Fort Washakie where 26 meets 287.

Campground

Dickinson Creek Campground, with 15 sites, is located at the end of the road mentioned above. Though most of the access road is in the Wind River Indian Reservation, the last 3 miles are in the National Forest. The Dickinson Park Ranger Station is located about a mile before the campground, and information and permits can be obtained there.

Hikes

The area discussed here is all shown on the Moccasin Lake 15′ U.S.G.S. quadrangle. Those considering trips to the west over the Divide will also want the Mt. Bonneville 15′ map. These are both rather old maps, but they are adequate. Some other regions in the Wind Rivers are still not included in normal U.S.G.S. series, but preliminary sheets can be obtained for some of the region if correspondence with the Survey is begun a few months in advance. There are excellent aerial photos in Bonney's *Guide to the Wyoming Mountains*.

Shoshone Lake—14 miles; 2200 feet. An old road leads southeast across Dickinson Park, connecting with the Shoshone Trail, which climbs a couple of hundred feet to the top of a rise and then drops down to the North Fork of the Popo Agie River. The Shoshone Trail then crosses to the other side of the river and climbs up the hill to the southeast to reach the lake.

North Fork Popo Agie River—6 miles; 1200 feet. Follow the Shoshone Trail (above) down to the river for a pleasant short walk.

Smith Lake—12 miles; 1850 feet. From the end of the road, the Smith Lake Trail heads southwest up a drainage, over a ridge, and down into the Smith Lake Creek valley. Smith Lake is 1¼ miles upstream. It is the lowest of a lovely group of lakes running up a spectacular pair of cirques, which give the flavor of the Wind Rivers and are much closer than the peaks along the Divide.

Middle Lake—13 miles; 2100 feet. A little further up the trail from Smith Lake.

Smith Lake Circuit—15 miles; 2300 feet. Where the trail described above comes into Smith Lake Creek from the north, another climbs up to the south, dropping after a couple of miles into High Meadow Creek and following it down to the North Fork of the Popo Agie. By using this trail for the return trip, the Smith Lake hike can be made into a circuit. The North Fork is followed downstream until the Shoshone Trail is met, which leads north back to Dickinson Creek Campground.

Middle Lake Circuit—17 miles; 2550 feet. The above route is used, but the trail followed past Smith Lake to the higher Middle Lake.

Backpacking Trips

Lonesome Lake—32 miles; 2700 feet. Since this lake is at the base of one of the most spectacular ring of peaks in the country, the Cirque of the Towers, it is well worth the trip, but since it is also a popular base camp for rock climbers, it is best for backpackers to make camp elsewhere and to walk up to the Cirque for a day trip. One can, for example, climb up to Bear Lake, north of the Lonesome Lake Trail, a couple of miles below Lonesome Lake, and find a campsite with no one else around. Begin by following the trail described for Shoshone Lake. Instead of following the Shoshone Trail up the south bank of the North Fork Popo Agie, take the Lonesome Lake Trail up the North Fork all the way to the lake. Return the same way.

Grave Lake Circuit—45 miles; 5400 feet. (*With side trips*—65 miles; 10,000 feet.) Take the Lonesome Lake Trail as described above. At Lizard Head Meadows, a couple of miles below Lonesome Lake, the Lizard Head Trail turns uphill to the right. The route follows this trail, and packs can be left here if the party chooses to make the worthwhile side trip on up to Lonesome Lake. With the Cirque of the Towers in view, it will be hard to resist. The Lizard Head Trail is much fainter than the Lonesome Lake Trail, but with some care is not too hard to follow. A side trail cuts lower to Bear Lake, which makes a good campsite. The trail now climbs high out of the valley, and there are excellent views as it proceeds north. It is about 8 miles before it meets the Bears' Ears Trail, soon after passing west of Cathedral Peak. Turn left on the Bears' Ears Trail and follow it down Valentine Creek, past Valentine Lake, down

A typical high-mountain face in the Rockies. Thousands of miles of trails lead to glaciated rock walls like this one, and permanent snowfields linger through the summer, feeding the lakes and streams below. This is the Medicine Bow Diamond, in Wyoming's Snowy Range.

into the canyon of the South Fork of the Little Wind River, which the trail then crosses. This crossing may be difficult, and if it cannot be managed, take the Bears' Ears Trail back to Dickinson Lake. Assuming the crossing can be made, the route proceeds down the South Fork. Upriver is a good side trip to Washakie Lake, 2½ miles and a few hundred feet. It is another couple of miles and 1300 feet to Washakie Pass, on the Continental Divide just north of Washakie Peak. From the crossing of the South Fork it is about 3 miles to Grave Lake. A side trip should be taken on up the trail a couple of miles to get a good view of the tremendous face of Mount Hooker, just off the map in this book. One can also climb to Hailey Pass on the Divide, 1200 feet above Grave Lake. To return, retrace the route to the junction with the Lizard Head Trail, and follow the Bears' Ears Trail back to Dickinson Creek Campground.

MEDICINE BOW MOUNTAINS— THE SNOWY RANGE

This is a beautiful little mountain area in southern Wyoming. It is not a major chain of peaks, nor is it deep and inaccessible wilderness. It is simply a delightful and unspoiled little alpine region with impressive faces and lovely lakes close to the road, where one can go hiking, climbing, fishing, or where one can sit watching the reflections of the peaks in the lakes below.

The nomenclature of these mountains is somewhat confused. The Medicine Bow Mountains form the Front Range in southern Wyoming and northern Colorado. They are not particularly high and, for the most part, not very rugged. The Colorado portion of the range is also called the Rawah Range. The Snowy Range is usually used to refer to the short section of precipitous peaks discussed in this book.

Approaches

From Interstate 80 take Wyoming State Route 130. If one is coming from the east, the turnoff is just past Laramie, and if one is driving from the west, it is 20 miles past Rawlins. Route 130 parallels the Interstate to the south, going over Snowy Range Pass, passing quite close to the mountains themselves.

Campgrounds

Several campgrounds are shown on the map. The most convenient to the scenery and the trails are Mirror Lake, with 12 sites, and Lewis Lake, with 16. Mirror Lake is about 14 miles beyond Centennial (coming from the east), while the turnoff for Lewis Lake is about 12 miles from Centennial. Brooklyn Lake and Silver Lake, the locations of which are shown on the map, have 15 and 21 sites respectively.

Hikes

Most of the best hiking in the Snowy Range is found by simply wandering around from one lake to another. The vegetation is scattered enough so that it is always simple enough to find a route, and one can easily spend whatever time is available wandering about. Most of the routes through the cliff bands require mountaineering experience, and novices should be careful not to get themselves into trouble. The ridge along the top of the Range is broad and safe, however, and there are fine views for hikers from all along it. The back side (northwest) is gentle, and hikers or backpackers can wander down to lakes on that side with no difficulty.

Range Circuit—7 miles; 2100 feet. This is probably most pleasant when done from the southwest end of the range. A trail works up from the west side of Lake Marie, switchbacking up the grass slopes to the left of the last cliffs. On attaining the ridge, the trail climbs over the successive summits with spectacular views down to the lakes below, culminating on the highest point, Medicine Bow Peak, 12,013 feet. The southeast side of

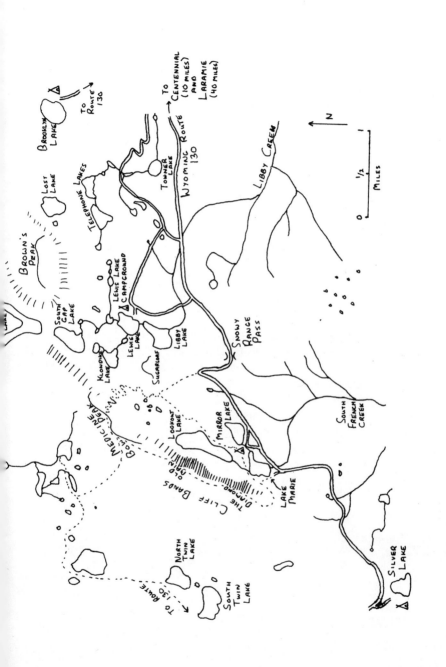

Medicine Bow is not as precipitous as that of some of the lesser summits, and a trail winds down it. Return to Mirror Lake Campground can be made by a trail which goes along the shore of Lookout Lake, with beautiful reflected views of the faces. Map: Medicine Bow Peak, 7½ '.

Backpacking Trips

The Snowy Range is not large enough for extended backpacking trips in the summer, but pleasant short jaunts can be made. A short walk away from the road will bring one to any number of pleasant campsites from which hikes can be made. The traverse of the range described above, or a longer one following the mountains further to the northeast, can be made into a two-day backpack. (The longer trip would require the addition of the Sand Lake 7½ ' quadrangle.)

Medicine Bow Peak-Heart Lake-Twin Lakes Circuit—12 miles; 2500 or 3000 feet. Begin by climbing Medicine Bow Peak as in the Range Circuit hike. Heart Lake can be seen to the north of the peak, but the easiest way down is west. In the valley the trail is picked up which goes east a mile to Heart Lake, a good camping spot. Follow this trail back west past Dipper Lake and south to the Twin Lakes. From here the trail continues south to meet State Route 130, and a left-hand turn takes one back a few miles to the campground. An alternate return route, requiring the larger altitude gain, is to go east from the Twin Lakes, following gentle slopes back up to the Range Crest, and taking either of the routes described in the Range Circuit back down. Map: Medicine Bow Peak, 7½ '.

CHAPTER 8

Trips in Utah

UINTA MOUNTAINS

THE UINTA MOUNTAINS form a beautiful range of high peaks in the northeastern corner of Utah, though they are not well-known by many hikers and backpackers outside that state. They are well worth the trip. Many peaks of the range exceed 13,000 feet, and the surrounding country receives plenty of snow in the winter, so the forests and meadows are well watered.

The Uintas are easy to get to from the Interstate system, but they are not crowded, and there are dozens of campsites which can be reached from either the north or south side of the range. The crest runs generally east and west with ridges running out to the north and south. There are many long valleys coming in from north and south, ending in lakes and cirques at the base of the high peaks, with occasional passes going across the crest or connecting adjoining valleys. The section covered here is at the western end of the range.

Approaches

The area of the Uintas covered in this book is approached by Utah State Route 150. If coming from the west, take Interstate 80 east from Salt Lake City about 35 miles to Wanship. Take Alternate U.S. 189 south 10 miles to Kamas, from which take State 150. It is 34 miles from Kamas to Hayden Pass, shown on the accompanying map.

Coming from the east, get off Interstate 80 at Evanston, Wyoming, taking State 150 south across the Utah border. It is about 34 miles to the turnoff for Christmas Meadows Campground.

Campgrounds

There are a number of campgrounds along Route 150. The ones closest to the trail system covered here are shown on the accompanying map. Christmas Meadows is probably the best. It is about 4 miles down a Forest Service road from the main highway on the Stillwater Fork and has 12 campsites. Most of the trails listed leave from there. Hayden Fork Campground has 8 sites, Beaver View has 20, and Butterfly has 16.

Hikes

FROM CHRISTMAS MEADOWS:

Amethyst Lake—12 miles; 2000 feet. Christmas Meadows lie in the lower part of the valley of the Stillwater Fork. Higher up, the valley splits in two, and the peaks rise on either side of each fork. Take the trail up the valley and take the eastern fork into lovely Amethyst Basin, containing the lake of the same name. Return the same way. Map: Whitney Reservoir, 7½'.

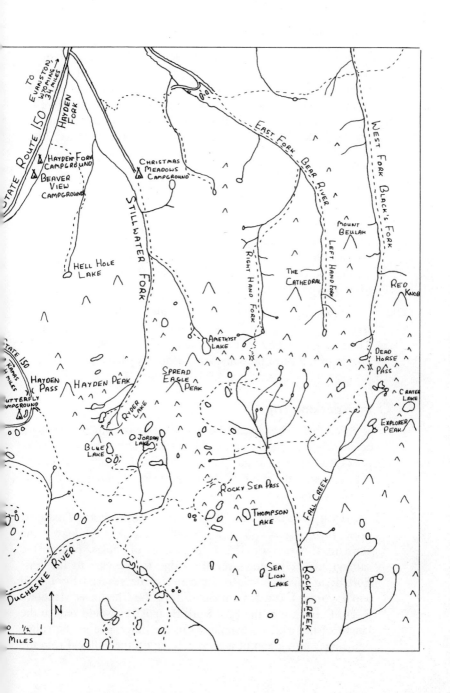

Ryder Lake—19 miles; 1900 feet. The western fork of the Stillwater Fork is somewhat longer. Take the trail upstream from Christmas Meadows for a couple of miles, until the trail splits, and take the western fork. At the cirque in the head of the canyon are several lakes, the trail leading to Ryder. Return the same way. Maps: Whitney Reservoir, 7½ '; Hayden Peak, 7½ '.

FROM HAYDEN PASS:

Blue Lake—11 miles; 1000 feet. From the parking area near Hayden Pass, on the other side of the road from Butterfly Campground, a trail goes southeast, along the south side of the crest. About 3½ miles along this trail, a side trail turns left up into a cirque. A mile further on, the trail splits again, the left-hand fork climbing up to Blue Lake. Return the same way. Map: Hayden Peak, 7½ '.

Jordan and Schuler Lakes—12 miles; 1000 feet. From the trail going to Blue Lake take the right-hand trail at the last fork. The trail goes past Jordan Lake and climbs to Schuler, a smaller lake above. Return the same way. Map: Hayden Peak, 7½ '.

Backpacking Trips

Any of the hikes listed above make fine overnight trips, with beautiful campsites near the high lakes. Other possible back-packs lead up the various parallel valleys. The longer trip listed below crosses the crest of the range twice, making a circuit of several valleys.

Circuit Trip-West Fork Black's Fork-Dead Horse Pass-East Fork Bear River—36 miles; 5000 feet. A trail leaves the Christmas Meadows Road a couple of miles before the campground, climbing over the ridge to the east to the East Fork Bear River. (This point can also be reached by a road leaving State 150 a few miles north of the Christmas Meadows Road. Driving into the East Fork Bear River would reduce the length of the trip to 26 miles.) On the other side of the ridge, one comes to the end of a road coming up the valley. From the

A typical Rocky Mountain trail winding up through the subalpine zone towards a pass on the Continental Divide.

other side another trail is followed over the next ridge into the West Fork Black's Fork valley. The route then follows the trail up the West Fork Black's Fork to Dead Horse Pass at its head. The trail then drops into the Fall Creek drainage to the south, contours west around the drainage, and follows a right-hand fork up over a ridge to the head of Rock Creek. (A lower fork contours around to meet Rock Creek at a lower elevation.) The route then winds around crossing several tributaries of Rock Creek. About 2½ miles after crossing into the Rock Creek drainage, a trail is followed which branches off to the right, climbing over a pass and dropping down to the right-hand fork of the East Fork Bear River. The trail is followed down-stream to the roadhead, from which one can take the path back over the ridge to Christmas Meadows. Maps: Whitney Reservoir, 7½'; Red Knob, 7½'; Explorer Peak, 7½'; Hayden Peak, 7½'.

CHAPTER 9

Trips in Colorado

NORTH PARK RANGE—
MOUNT ZIRKEL WILDERNESS

THE MOUNT ZIRKEL Wilderness extends for about 25 miles north and south along the Continental Divide in Colorado, just south of the Wyoming border. The mountains in this section are lower than those further south, the highest ones reaching a little over 12,000 feet. This is a particularly beautiful section of the Colorado Rockies, however, with well-watered forests extending up to lovely lakes and alpine tundra covered with wild flowers. Fishing is excellent. Some of the mountains in the area are gentle and flat-topped, while others like the Sawtooths, Big Agnes, and Zirkel itself present some very rugged features. Roads, campgrounds, and some trails are shown on the Forest Service map of Routt and White River National Forests. The ranger station is in Steamboat Springs.

Approaches

The Mount Zirkel Wilderness is north of Rabbit Ears Pass on U.S. 40. It can be approached from the east or the west from either Colorado or Wyoming. One campground is listed here on the east side, but the recommended approach is from Steamboat Springs and Clark, Colorado, to the fine campgrounds on the west side of the wilderness along the Elk River. Just up the road from these campgrounds, the trails start from the old mining camp of Slavonia.

Campgrounds

Big Creek Lakes: From Cowdrey, east of the wilderness, take county road 6W west. The road turns to gravel about a mile out of town. It is about 17 miles to the turnoff left up the South Fork of Big Creek, and another 6 or 7 miles to the campground on the shore of the larger lake. There are 45 campsites, and drinking water is available.

Hinman (13 sites), *Box Canyon* (11 sites), and *Seedhouse* (25 sites) are located along the Elk River road, west of the wilderness. After taking state route 129 north from Steamboat Springs about 17 miles, follow a good gravel road to the right, up the Elk River. The three campgrounds are along this road, the first being about 5 or 6 miles in, and the others a bit farther. Hinman and Seedhouse have drinking water. One should carry water to Box Canyon or purify the river water. The road ends at Slavonia, a couple of miles past Seedhouse campground.

Hikes

FROM SLAVONIA:

Gold Creek Lake—7 miles; 1200 feet. Take the Wyoming

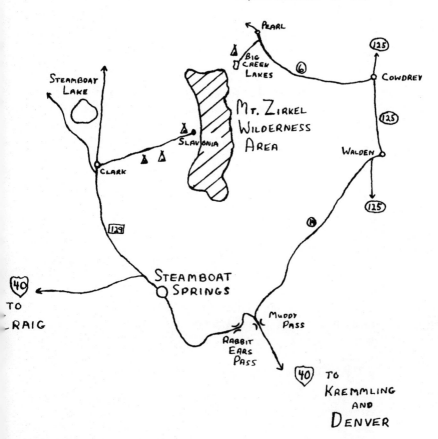

Trail, which starts from Slavonia on the south side of Gilpin Creek. The trail follows Gold Creek up to the lake. Maps: Mt. Zirkel, 7½′, or Pearl, 15′.

Gilpin Lake—7½ miles; 1900 feet. Take the Gilpin-Mica Basin Trail west from Slavonia, keeping to the right when the two separate in about a mile. The hike to this lovely lake is highly recommended. Maps: as above.

Mica Basin—7½ miles; 2000 feet. Begin as above, but follow the left-hand fork up Mica Creek to this spectacular basin below Big Agnes and the Sawtooths. Instead of crossing the creek at the basin where the trail starts to climb up, one can follow the creek an extra quarter-mile to Mica Lake. Maps: as above.

Gilpin Lake-Gold Creek Circuit—9½ miles; 2500 feet. Follow the description to Gilpin Lake. The trail then heads due south around the west side of the lake and crosses a small pass. It winds down the hillside, the trail from Red Dirt Pass comes in from the left, and one meets the Ute Pass trail at the creek in the bottom of the canyon. Turn right here and follow the trail past Gold Creek Lake and down to Slavonia. Maps: as above.

FROM SEEDHOUSE CAMPGROUND:

Three Island Lake—9 miles; 1800 feet. The trail is picked up by the river. Follow it upstream until a bridge is reached. The trail crosses the bridge, climbs a hill, and then turns left to follow a wooded ridge, nearly on the crest for a way. It then contours to the right to meet Three Island Creek and follows the creek to the lake. Maps: Farwell Mt., 7½′, and Pearl, 15′, or Mt. Zirkel, 7½′.

FROM BIG CREEK LAKES CAMPGROUND:

Seven Lakes—11 miles; 1800 feet. The trail can be picked up either by walking around the north and west sides of the larger lake or by going between the two lakes and along the north side of the smaller (south) one. The trail follows the main drainage system feeding the lakes past Big Creek Falls into the wilderness. It then goes through a meadow, climbs a long forested slope, and passes above Lake Eileen. It turns south and meets the Buffalo Ridge Trail ¼ mile before reaching the lakes. Maps: Pearl, 15′, or Pearl, 7½′, and Davis Pk., 7½′.

Two- or Three-Day Backpack

Ute Pass—21 miles; 5700 feet. Follow the Gilpin Trail from Slavonia to Gilpin Lake. Turn south, follow the trail around the

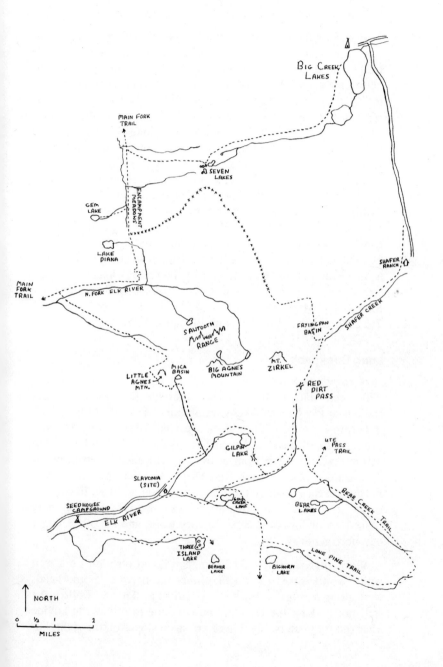

west side of the lake and over the pass. Follow the trail all the way down to the creek at the bottom of the canyon, passing the trail to Red Dirt Pass which comes in from the left ¼ mile before the creek. At Gold Creek turn left and follow the trail up to Ute Pass. At the top of the pass, follow the trail down to the right into the Bear Creek valley, instead of taking the Ute Pass Trail on up to the left. Follow the trail along Bear Creek for 3 miles, and turn right on the Lone Pine Trail about ½ mile after leaving the wilderness area. The trail climbs slightly and contours around a ridge to meet Lone Pine Creek. Follow the trail up the valley to the pass above, where it meets the Wyoming Trail. Turn right, and follow the trail down past Gold Creek Lake, along Gold Creek, and back to Slavonia. Good campsites can be found at Gilpin Lake, in the Gold Creek valley just before the trail begins the climb to Ute Pass, along Bear Creek, at the Bear Lakes, ½ mile west of the creek, along Lone Pine Creek, and at Bighorn Lake, ¼ west of the trail up the Lone Pine valley. Maps: Pearl, 15′, and Mt. Ethel, 15′, or Mt. Zirkel, 7½′, Boettcher Lake, 7½′, and Pitchpine Mtn., 7½′.

Long Backpack

Northern Peaks Circuit—28 miles; 8000 feet; or 41 miles; 8700 feet. Start at Slavonia. An alternate start for the longer route is at Big Creek Lakes Campground. Take the Gilpin Trail to Gilpin Lake, head around the west side of the lake and south over the small pass, and turn left on the Red Dirt Pass Trail before reaching the bottom of the valley. Follow the trail below an old mine and up over Red Dirt Pass, and drop down into Fryingpan Basin, where there is good camping. From Fryingpan Basin there are two possible routes, one shorter and more rugged, involving some cross-country work, and the other longer but more gentle.

Short, rugged route—At Fryingpan Basin turn left on a trail which works across the Basin, climbs the north side, and heads west along a ridge to meet the Continental Divide. Follow the trail north along the Divide, and continue to follow the Divide after the trail peters out. There are steep slopes on the right, but the top and left sides are gentle, so there are no real difficulties. After 5 miles along the crest, the Divide drops to a low pass at Encampment Meadows, and here the Main Fork Trail is met at the pass.

Long, gentler route—Continue along the Fryingpan Trail, which generally follows Shafer Creek. About 3 miles after the trail leaves the wilderness area, the Shafer Ranch is reached. Take the trail and gravel road north to Big Creek Lakes, about 7 miles distant. The Big Creek Trail then follows the watershed feeding the Lakes, past Big Creek Falls, Lake Eileen, and Seven Lakes. At Seven Lakes the route goes past the junction with the Buffalo Ridge Trail, crosses a pass, and drops down to meet the Main Fork Trail at the Encampment River. Turn left and head upstream 2 miles to Encampment Meadows, where the rough alternative route is joined. Lake Eileen can be used as an intermediate campsite.

Continuation of both routes—Camp can be made at Encampment Meadows or at Gem Lake, which is reached by following a side trail and creek joining the Main Fork Trail a mile north of the pass. Gem Lake is a mile and 500 feet above this junction. The route goes south from the pass and drops down to meet the North Fork of the Elk River. Follow the trail downriver until it meets the Mica Basin Trail at the confluence of the North Fork and Agnes Creek. Turn left and follow the Mica Basin Trail up Agnes Creek. The trail then works around Little Agnes Mountain, going up slightly, and reaches Mica Basin on the other side. Continue out the Mica Basin Trail to meet the Gilpin Trail about a mile from the starting point at Slavonia. There are plenty of good campsites all along this section of the trip. Maps: Farwell Mt., 7½', and Pearl, 15', or Mt. Zirkel, 7½', Boettcher Lake, 7½', Pearl, 7½', and Davis Pk., 7½'.

Further Comments on Backpacking

The routes suggested here concentrate on the northern and

more rugged section of the wilderness area. The peaks of the southern portion are less jagged, and it is particularly easy to pick routes along the rather flat crest. One should expect to meet quite a few signs of sheep grazing in those areas, however.

The fact that there is a good deal of use of the entire region for sheep pasture should make the backpacker cautious of his water supplies. Do not assume stream purity unless you have been up the whole watershed or it is so rugged that grazing higher up would be impossible. Naturally, water purification tablets should be carried in case they are needed.

Many high areas in this section of the Rockies are suitable for camping in good weather. If high camps are planned, however, a portable stove should be carried. Fires should never be built above the heavily forested regions, since wood grows too slowly in the higher zones.

GORE RANGE

The Gore Range is one of the most rugged areas in the Colorado Rockies, filled with jagged peaks and sawtoothed ridges. It is a fine wilderness which escaped the discovery of valuable minerals and hence the roads that were built to get at them. Though the rough part of the Range is not large enough nor far enough from major roads to be really difficult of access, the high lakes require hard backpacking or hiking to reach.

The Gores form a part of the main crest of the Colorado Rockies, more or less between the North Park Range and the Sawatch Range, separated from the Front Range to the east by Middle Park, a high, flat valley. The Continental Divide does not pass through the Gore Range—at this point it curves far to the east and runs down the crest of the Front Range above Denver. The Gores are far enough west to receive quite a bit of rain, and the woods there are fairly thick and high. At lower altitudes the Gore Range is full of beautiful forest coming down the steep sides of rushing creeks—spectacular and tough country.

Approaches

To approach the campground and trailhead recommended here for the Gore Range, take Colorado State Route 9 south from Kremmling on U.S. 40 or north from Dillon on Interstate 70. At Green Mountain Reservoir (which may not appear on older maps) a side road goes off to Heeney on the west side of the reservoir, opposite the side where Route 9 passes. From south of Heeney, a Forest Service road goes in about 3 miles to Lower Cataract Lake.

Campsite

The Cataract Creek Campground, near Lower Cataract Lake, has 7 campsites and drinking water.

Hikes

All of the Gore Range covered here is shown on the White River National Forest map, though much of the area is in Arapaho National Forest. Farther north, part of the Range is in Routt National Forest. The Forest Service map is not detailed enough to be of much use for hiking, however. Not all of the region has yet been remapped by the Geological Survey in the 7½ minute series, and where the old 15-minute editions are used, campers should remember that some are nearly fifty years old. Trails in particular have changed, though accuracy in this region is fairly good.

Surprise Lake Circuit—10 miles; 1850 feet. This pretty little lake is on the main Gore Range Trail, to which there are several methods of access from Lower Cataract Lake and Cataract Creek Campground, allowing various hikes with different return routes. The shortest route to the trail and the lake can be used to start this hike; it goes south from near the campground and meets the Gore Range Trail soon after crossing the stream feeding out of Surprise Lake. Those wanting a shorter hike (7 miles; 1400 feet) can return the same way. Otherwise, turn west

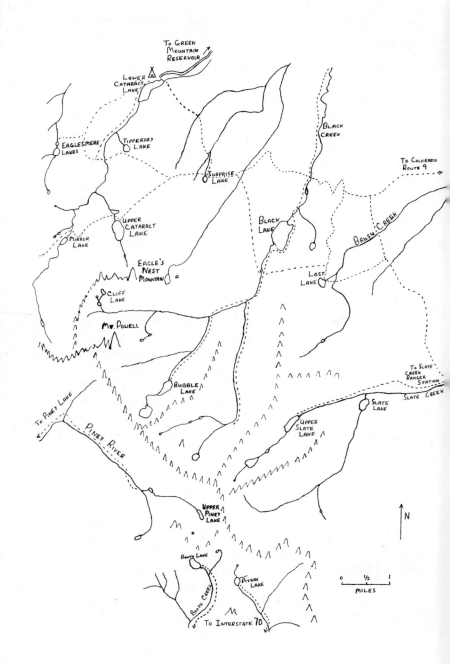

To Green
Mountain
Reservoir

Lower
Cataract
Lake

Black
Creek

Eaglesmere
Lakes

Tipperary
Lake

Surprise
Lake

To Colorado
Route 9

Upper
Cataract
Lake

Black
Lake

Brush Creek

Mirror
Lake

Eagle's
Nest
Mountain

Lost
Lake

Cliff
Lake

Mt. Powell

To Slate
Creek
Ranger
Station

Slate Creek

Bubble
Lake

Slate
Lake

Upper
Slate
Lake

To Piney Lake

Piney River

Upper
Piney
Lake

N

Booth Lake

0   ½   1
MILES

Booth Creek

Pitkin
Lake

To Interstate 70

on the Gore Range trail and then turn right at the junction for Lower Cataract ½-1 mile past Surprise Lake. The main trail climbs a ridge here, which it then descends to the lake. Shorter and rougher use trails follow the stream more closely. Note that the main Gore Range Trail no longer goes by Eaglesmere Lakes, as shown on the old U.S.G.S. Mt. Powell Quad. Instead, it goes on past Upper Cataract and Mirror Lakes. Map: Mt. Powell, 15′.

Upper Cataract Lake Circuit—13 miles; 2350 feet. Follow the route described above for Surprise Lake. On coming to the junction where the Gore Range Trail branches off left from the route back down to Lower Cataract Lake, take this left-hand fork on to the upper lake. On the return trip, the second route back to camp can be followed after reaching the fork. The big peak above the lake is Eagle's Nest Mountain. Map: Mt. Powell, 15′.

Mirror Lake Circuit—15 miles; 2550 feet. To lengthen the Upper Cataract Lake trip a little more, continue along the Gore Range Trail to the somewhat lower Mirror Lake before returning. Besides Eagle's Nest, Meridian Mountain can be seen at the head of the Mirror Lake watershed. Map: Mt. Powell, 15′.

Eaglesmere Lakes—7½ miles; 1900 feet. Begin from Lower Cataract Lake on the trail used for the return leg on the preceding three trips. It heads northwest uphill from near the campground. The trail climbs steadily for a couple of miles and then levels off a bit for about a mile as it works along near the top of the ridge. The old Gore Range Trail then branches off to the right and crosses the ridge to the Eaglesmere Lakes, while the new trail drops down to cross Cataract Creek. Follow the old trail about ¾ mile from the junction to reach the lakes. Map: Mt. Powell, 15′.

Backpacking Trips

All the hikes just listed can be used for moderate two-day

Peaceful trails and diverting streams are also to be found in abundance in the Rockies. Children find far more interest in a hike if they have some chance to play in the water.

backpacking routes. The longer trips listed below present more of a challenge.

Bubble Lake—20 miles; 3000 feet. This little lake is as cheerful as its name, but the surroundings are far more spectacular than one might guess. The jagged peaks of the Gore Range surround it, and since it is above timberline, the view is unobstructed. Most of the summits about are unnamed on the maps, though mountaineers have letter designations for them. From Cataract Creek Campground follow the trail described for Surprise Lake, and turn east on the Gore Range Trail. One soon comes to a branch, with one trail dropping down to the left to meet Black Creek below Black Lake, and the other contouring around to the right to intersect the creek at a much higher point; take the right fork. On reaching Black Creek, follow the trail which goes upstream. At the first major fork in the stream, about ¾ mile up, the main trail branches left. Take the right-hand fork and continue up unmaintained trails, keeping to the left at the next two stream forks and climbing steadily to the lake. There is another lake six hundred feet above Bubble, at the base of a snowfield rising up to the Continental Divide. This is a fairly rugged trip, not for the timid. Maps: Mt. Powell, 15', Vail East, 7½'.

East Fork of Black Creek—25 miles; 3000 feet. This trip goes into the next cirque east from Bubble Lake. It is incorrectly labelled Brush Creek on the old Mt. Powell Quad, Brush Creek being a separate, nearby drainage. Follow the directions for Bubble Lake until the first fork is reached on the way up Black Creek, where the trail up the left fork should be followed. There are good campsites in the high valley just below the timberline, above which there are several pretty lakes. Maps: Mt. Powell, 15'; Vail East, 7½'.

Upper Slate Lake—35 miles; 5600 feet. This is another spectacular cirque, reached by a good trail, the next one east from the East Fork of Black Creek. A series of small lakes, of which Upper Slate is the largest, runs up the canyon between two sawtooth ridges. Hike up to the Gore Range Trail near Surprise

Lake (see the first hike for the route) and then follow the trail east for about 9 miles to Slate Creek. Take the trail up Slate Creek to the lake. Maps: Mt. Powell, 15′, Ute Peak, 15′, Dillon, 15′, Vail East, 7½′.

Variations from Colorado Route 9—All three of the back-packing routes mentioned can be done from starts at Green Mountain Reservoir or the state road. A dirt road goes up Black Creek from the road on the south side of the reservoir, near the east end. Driving up the road to Black Lake will cut about 8 miles off the trip to either Bubble Lake or the East Fork of Black Creek, but if you have to walk the road, the distance will be about the same as from Cataract Creek Campground. About 4 miles southeast of the Reservoir on Colorado Route 9 is the Slate Creek Ranger Station. The trail up Slate Creek starts from here and if the backpack is done from this point it will be 17 miles; 2800 feet.

FLATTOPS

The Flattops are rather different than most of the areas presented in this book. They are in the western part of Colorado, west of the Gore Range. The region has been lifted up like the crest of the Rockies, but shows little evidence of large-scale buckling and glaciation. Deep river valleys have been cut here and there, but in between there are many large tablelands, dotted with hundreds of lakes and heavily forested.

The Flattops are quite wild—the area is a proposed wilder-ness—but because it is less rugged than many neighboring areas, it is ideal hiking and backpacking country for families with small children. There is fine fishing in many of the lakes and streams.

Approaches

The hikes and backpacking trips listed here leave from

Trapper's Lake Campground. There are several ways to reach Trapper's Lake, but perhaps the simplest is from Meeker. From Interstate 70 at Rifle take State Route 13-789 north, or from U.S. Route 40 at Craig, take the same road south to Meeker. From a couple of miles east of Meeker, State Route 132 goes into the Flattops, passing ranger stations at Buford and Lost Creek, and turning into a Forest Service Road before reaching Trapper's Lake about 46 miles from Meeker. The campgrounds shown at the south end of the map can be reached from Dotsero, east of Glenwood Springs on Interstate 70.

Campgrounds

The campground recommended is at Trapper's Lake, and it has 51 campsites. Trails are described as leading from there, but the other campsites shown on the map also connect with the trail system as indicated. Himes Peak Campground has 8 sites; Heart Lake has 3; Deep Lake has 12. There are other campgrounds further out along each of the approach roads, but these are less convenient to the trail system.

Hikes

There are so many small and delightful lakes sprinkled through the Flattops that walking off for a mile or two on almost any trail will lead to one of them. The many lakes are one of the special features that makes hiking in this area so enjoyable. Trapper's Lake itself is nestled in an amphitheatre below the plateau, so all the trails leading from it begin by climbing up one of the streams to the relatively level area above. The peaks shown on the map are prominences which rise above the plateau around, but they are not of great height.

The Flattops area is not yet mapped on either 7½ or 15-minute quadrangles. The hikes and backpacking trips listed here are all covered by the Glenwood Springs 30-minute quad, but in using it remember that trails have changed somewhat since it was made in 1927.

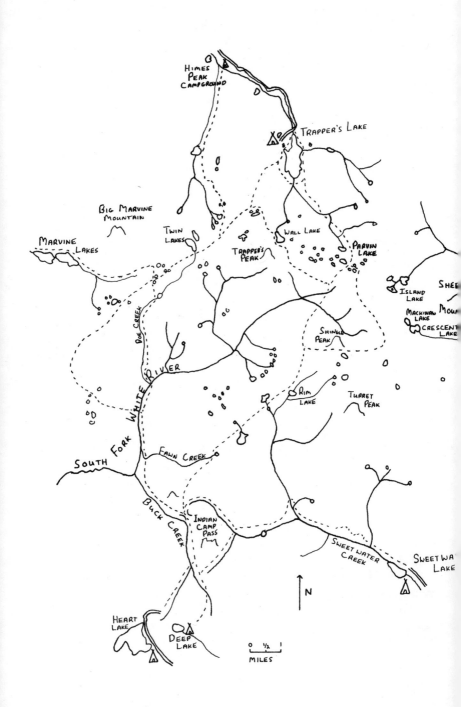

Wall Lake—8 miles; 1400 feet. Take the trail which goes around the west side of Trapper's Lake and follows the stream feeding in from the southwest uphill. It attains the rim by a group of pretty little lakes perhaps 2½ miles from the campground. Take the left fork at these lakes and follow the trail over to Wall Lake, which is at the head of another stream feeding down to Trapper's.

Trapper's Lake Circuit—4 miles; 300 feet. Trails lead around Trapper's Lake itself, and the circuit is a pleasant walk.

Parvin Lake—9 miles; 1100 feet. Take the trail following the stream coming into Trapper's Lake from the southeast. It is most easily reached by walking down the east side of the lake. Parvin Lake is up the canyon, a few hundred feet below the rim.

Wall Lake-Parvin Lake Circuit—12 miles; 1900 feet. Continue following the trail past Wall Lake, under the slopes of Trapper's Peak. After a couple of miles of gentle uphill walking, another trail will be reached, and a left-hand turn will take the hiker down past Parvin Lake and back towards the campground.

Twin Lakes—10 miles; 1400 feet. Begin on the same trail as the one for Wall Lake. At the lakes on the rim turn right instead of left, crossing a gentle saddle, and coming down into a basin full of small lakes. On the other side of these small lakes are the larger and somewhat higher Twin Lakes.

Backpacking Trips

Marvine Lakes—22 miles; 3100 feet. These lakes lie in another side canyon below the rim. Begin the hike by following the trail to Twin Lakes. Continue along the trail from Twin Lakes over another two miles of relatively flat terrain. At another group of small lakes the trail to Marvine Lakes branches off to the right and follows a canyon down to the Marvine Lakes. Return by the same route.

Shingle Peak Circuit—20 miles; 2500 feet. Follow the directions given in the Wall Lake-Parvin Lake Circuit hike until the trail junction 2 miles past Wall Lake is reached. Turn right here, following fairly level terrain as the trail heads towards Shingle Peak. The trail passes the peak on the right, at the end of a long, gentle ridge. Just after the trail rounds the end of the ridge, a trail branches off to the left, going around the mountain, while the main trail goes straight. Take the left-hand trail. Several trails go off to the right in the next couple of miles, but continue taking the left forks around the mountain. Finally the trail heads back north and meets the Parvin Lake trail, which is followed back to Trapper's Lake.

White River Circuit—35 miles; 3500 feet. The biggest drainage from the Flattops Plateau is the White River. This circuit crosses the Flattops, drops down into the canyon of the South Fork of the White River, and then climbs back up and crosses back by a different route. Begin by following the trail to Twin Lakes, as described in the "Hikes" section. Beyond Twin Lakes, where the trail comes in from Marvine Lakes to the right, there is a fork, with two trails going ahead, one slightly right and staying high, and the other slightly left, dropping down Doe Creek. Either can be taken. The Doe Creek Trail drops down to the White River right away, while the other continues on the plateau for a couple of miles before dropping down to the left. The White River is met in an area known as the Meadows. Continue down the White for a couple of miles after the two trails rejoin, and then follow the trail left which goes up Buck Creek. A couple of miles up Buck Creek there is a three-way trail junction called Indian Camp Pass. One trail continues up Buck Creek, a second goes left over a small saddle into the Sweetwater Creek drainage, and the third, which our route follows, climbs the shoulder to the left back up onto the plateau. This trail continues past Shingle Peak and Parvin Lake back to the campground.

SAWATCH RANGE—
MOUNT HOLY CROSS REGION

The Sawatch Range is a large group of mountains in the central Colorado Rockies, running north and south for a distance of almost one hundred miles. It is a high range, with 15 peaks rising over 14,000 feet and scores over 13,000. It extends from the general area of Eagle in the north to the head of the San Luis Valley in the south, and it is crossed by Independence, Cottonwood, and Hagerman Passes, at intervals along its length. Administratively, the Sawatch Range is in White River and San Isabel National Forests. Such a large range naturally offers many opportunities for campers and hikers, among which it is rather difficult to choose.

Mount Holy Cross, which is just over 14,000 feet high, was once very widely known for the cross of snow formed by permanent fields lying in its northeast couloir and a horizontal shelf near the top of the mountain. Longfellow wrote a poem about the mountain, and copies of photographs and paintings of it still circulate widely. It was once a National Religious Monument, and many pilgrims came from some distance for a view. In these more secular times, its official status has long since been dropped, and the cross itself sometimes melts completely away during some summers. The country and the mountain are as beautiful and enduring as ever, though, and there are many fine hikes around and on the Mountain of the Holy Cross.

Approaches

The Holy Cross area is south of Interstate 70, just west of Vail. Take 70 to U.S. 24 and turn south towards Minturn and Leadville; this junction is about 110 miles west of Denver and about 5 miles west of Vail. Travel approximately 4½ miles south, through Minturn, past a Ranger Station (where you can get a map of White Mountain National Forest) and Battle Mountain High School, and turn right on the Half Moon

Campground Road. If you cross the bridge to the east side of the Eagle River, you have just missed the road. The road is a good dirt one, about 7½ miles long.

Campgrounds

There are two campgrounds on the approach road mentioned above. About 5½ or 6 miles up the road is Tigiwon Campground, with 9 campsites. At the end of the road, another 2½ miles on, is Half Moon Campground, with 7 sites. Both have drinking water.

Hikes

Two 7½' U.S.G.S. topographic maps cover all the hikes mentioned here: Minturn and Mount of the Holy Cross.

View of the Cross—7 miles; 2800 feet. Take the well-marked trail from Half Moon Campground to Notch Mountain. The best view of the famous cross is from the notch for which this mountain is named, where there is an old shelter that was built for pilgrims. The trail travels an easy 2 miles along the hillside before beginning the climb up the mountain. On Mount Holy Cross, there is a second snowfield which is known as the Supplicating Virgin. Below her is a large lake, called the Bowl of Tears.

Lake Constantine—8 miles; 1100 feet. This pretty lake is reached by starting on the same easy trail that leads towards Notch Mountain. After 2 miles there is a trail junction, with the trail up the mountain going right and the trail to Lake Constantine, Hunky Dory Lake, and Holy Cross City going left. Another 2 miles brings the hiker to the lake.

Tuhare Lakes—12 miles; 2100 feet. These spectacular lakes above Lake Constantine can be reached by some rugged, cross-country scrambling after 5 miles of easy trail hiking. Continue for about a mile past the spot where the trail first comes to the north end of Lake Constantine. The trail climbs above the lake

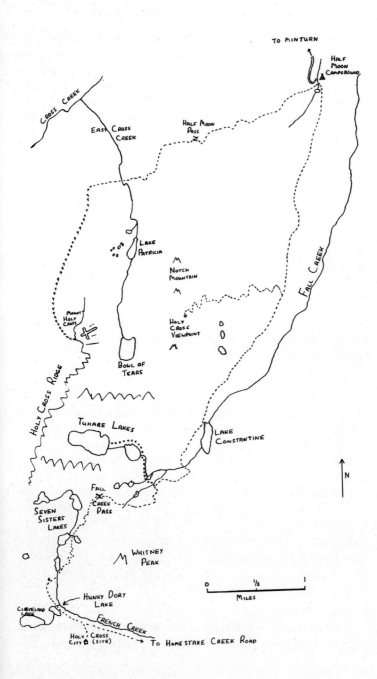

for a while, then crosses the stream feeding the lake. Shortly after getting out of the woods, the trail comes back to the stream and climbs up the hill with it before veering left up the hill. Turn right when the trail veers, cross the stream, and contour around a few hundred yards to a small lakelet on another branch of the stream. Take the northernmost of the two creeks feeding the lakelet, and follow it up to the Tuhare Lakes, beautiful and icy in their cirque below the Holy Cross Ridge.

Half Moon Pass—3 miles; 1400 feet. This pass crosses the northern ridge of Notch Mountain, giving access to East Cross Creek and the ridge by which Mount Holy Cross is most easily climbed. It makes a pleasant walk with a nice view. A second trail also starts from Half Moon Campground, starting on the west side of the little creek that flows by the campground, and climbing up the hill. The pass is 1½ miles away, a little above timberline.

East Cross Creek—6 miles; 2300 feet. Continue along the trail that goes over Half Moon Pass, following it down into the watershed of this creek.

Lake Patricia—6 miles; 2000 feet. The most obvious way to reach Lake Patricia is by following the trail just discussed down to East Cross Creek and working up the creek bed. This turns out to be a generally unpleasant bushwhack, however, and a better way is to leave the trail about ⅜ mile beyond the pass, contouring around the northwestern slope of Notch Mountain, past a huge and prominent boulder, and eventually picking up a line of cairns which take one high on the ridge and then down a shelf to the slopes above the lake. This is a tricky cross-country route and should not be attempted by the inexperienced or those who do not have a sense for routefinding. Those going around Lake Patricia should choose the west shore. There are nice campsites on the west and north benches of the lake.

Bowl of Tears—8 miles; 2600 feet. Also not for novices. From

Lake Patricia, follow the stream course up through the boulders and over the rise to the south.

Backpacking Trips

Several of the hikes above make nice backpacking trips. One can pack in to Lake Patricia and camp, for example, and then take day hikes the following day to Tuhare Lakes and other spots in the area. A couple of slightly longer trips are suggested here which will take average hikers two or three days.

Mount Holy Cross Climb—10 miles; 5600 feet. Follow the route described above to East Cross Creek. There are some nice campsites a little above the trail there. For the climb, continue up out of the creek to the ridge which rises on the other side of it all the way to the top of the mountain. This is a cross-country route, but it is not difficult, apart from the physical effort required to climb to 14,000 feet. The final part of the route goes up the west slope of the mountain, avoiding the northern cirque. Packs can be left at camp on East Cross Creek, except for emergency gear, water, and food.

Holy Cross City—18 miles; 4300 feet. This is a beautiful trip past many lovely lakes to the old mining town of Holy Cross City, deserted soon after it was built in the 19th century. There are many little side trips possible along this route, and fishermen should like its proximity to streams and lakes. Follow the route mentioned above for Lake Constantine. Continue on up the trail over Fall Creek Pass, and drop down past the Seven Sisters Lakes to Hunky Dory Lake, the terminus of a rough jeep track from the other side. A little past Hunky Dory Lake on the jeep track, a fork to the right will take you up the hill to the ghost town. Before heading back, you may want to explore some of the short side trails around the old mines (stay out!), to Cleveland Lake, the Mulhall Lakes, and Fancy Lakes. Whitney Peak is an easy climb from Fall Creek Pass.

SAN JUAN MOUNTAINS

The San Juans are the great C-shaped range which stands in the southwestern part of Colorado. The Continental Divide makes a great bend along the crest of the San Juans. The group is so large that over a dozen sub-ranges are included in it. Both the structure and character of the region is varied. There are peaks of granite and mountains composed of sedimentary rock. Some of the mountains have striking vertical faces, and others are piles of rubble. Much of the country is laced with jeep roads, while other sections are wild and very difficult to get into.

Lovers of old mining towns will want to spend some time sightseeing in the San Juan region, because much of this area was heavily mined, and some of it still is. This part of Colorado has not seen the development boom that has taken place on the east slope of the Rockies, and much of the mining country remains pretty much as it has been for decades.

Mining has opened much of this country with jeep roads, which often make things less interesting for those hikers who do not have four-wheel-drive vehicles. The section of the San Juans chosen here is an exception, however. It can be reached only by narrow-gauge railroad or by many miles on the trail.

The Needles area of the San Juans, the region covered in this book, is in the San Juan National Forest. It has a number of peaks over 14,000 feet high, and only a few trails penetrate it. The narrow-gauge railroad that is normally used to get to the trailhead runs regularly from late May to early October, and in the off-season access is very difficult indeed. The combination of the train ride with the rugged wilderness of the Needles makes this a particularly rewarding trip.

Just as there are not many ways to get into the Needles area, the trail system within it is quite limited. The trails that are shown on the accompanying map are in good condition and are easy to find, but those attempting to make their way up other streams or over passes in the region should be experienced and

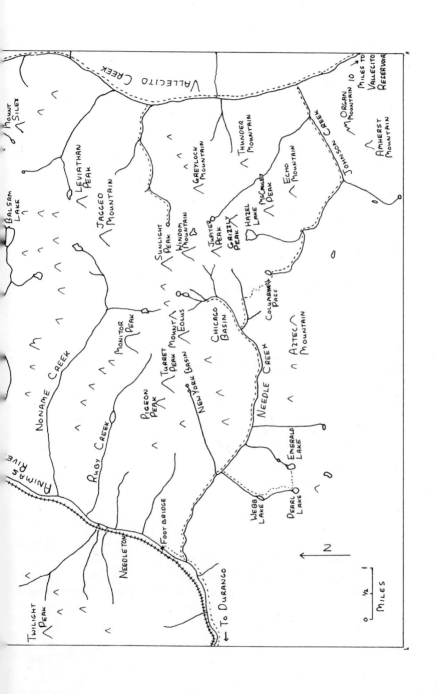

take care to keep track of their position on the map. Much of this country is real wilderness.

Despite overall ruggedness, however, beginners should not hesitate to travel to this area. The route up to Chicago Basin, in whole or in part, is a unique opportunity for getting far from the nearest road with only a moderate amount of hiking.

Approaches

The recommended way into the Needles is via the Durango-Silverton train, the last regularly scheduled narrow-gauge passenger train operating in the United States. The train ride itself is quite enjoyable and is a popular tourist attraction. For this reason, reservations should be made in advance, including notification of the desired stop. Write to the Denver & Rio Grande Ticket Office, Durango, Colorado 81301. Schedules and ticket prices may vary from year to year, but in the past one train has run in each direction from early May to early October, with an additional train following the first during midsummer. Trains have left Durango at 8:30 A.M. (second train, if any, at 9:30), and the return train from Silverton in midafternoon. Passengers can board at either end. Ticket prices have been under $10.

For the trips recommended in this book, notify the railroad of a desired stop at Needleton. Remind the conductor when you board the train. There is a Forest Service footbridge across the Animas River near Needleton, approximately ½ mile above the mouth of Needle Creek. Stops at the higher creeks can also be arranged, but usually only on the return trip from Silverton. Getting to these creeks requires fording the Animas, which is only possible in low water, late in the summer. Earlier, getting to Noname or Tenmile Creek requires unpleasant bushwhacking up from the footbridge at Needleton.

The other access shown on the map is via the Vallecito Creek Trail from Vallecito Reservoir. Take U.S. Route 160 east from Durango 20 miles to Bayfield and a county road north to the reservoir. It is 14 miles to the reservoir and another 6 miles to the end of the road at the north end.

Campgrounds

If the train is taken to Needleton, there are no formal campgrounds, though many good places to camp can be found along the Animas and Needle Creek. Campers going this way should be able to backpack their equipment for at least a couple of miles, however. Water from the side creeks here is quite safe, though water from the Animas should probably be boiled or chemically treated.

There are a number of campgrounds around Vallecito Reservoir, but the most suitable for trips into the wilderness is Vallecito Campground, with 44 sites, located on Vallecito Creek beyond the head of the reservoir. The Vallecito Creek Trail leaves from this campground.

Hikes

Most of the possible destinations in the Needles themselves will be reached by backpacking, because if one comes in by train, equipment must be backpacked anyhow, and the approach from Vallecito Reservoir is rather long for most day hikes. Short hikes up Vallecito Creek are rewarding in themselves, however, with good views of some of the peaks. Fishing is reasonably good, particularly in some of the tributaries.

Hikers from Vallecito Creek will want the Vallecito Reservoir 7½′ quadrangle as well as the map mentioned below for the Needles area proper.

Backpacking Trips

All backpacking trips from Needleton are covered by the old Needle Mountains 15′ quadrangle. This map is generally adequate, but it was made in 1900, and the trails shown are often inaccurate. The northern half of this map has been redone recently in 7½′ sections, Snowdon Peak and Storm King Peak, which would be useful for those planning trips in the drainages of Tenmile Creek, Noname Creek, Ruby Creek, or the northern part of the Vallecito Creek drainage. The trips suggested here, however, are on the southern part of the Needle Mountain map, which has not been redone.

The Needles are rugged, and it is well not to plan to make very long hikes each day, particularly if any cross-country travel is planned. Most of the passes require a good deal of route-finding and can often not be crossed without mountaineering skills and equipment. (Columbine Pass has a good trail and is not difficult.) Crossing the larger streams, particularly the Animas and Vallecito Creek, in spring and early summer can be difficult or impossible except at bridges. The bridge near Needleton across the Animas has been mentioned. The Vallecito Creek Trail crosses a bridge from the south side of the creek about a mile off the accompanying map, so if the Vallecito is too high for crossing at Johnson Creek, it can be followed south to the bridge.

Besides the trips mentioned here, good circuits can be made in either direction between Needleton and the Vallecito Reservoir if a car shuttle is arranged or if someone can hitch a ride between Durango and the reservoir. Experienced and ambitious cross-country hikers could go up Tenmile Creek (there is a rough cairned route), cross the pass between Mount Silex and Storm King Peak, go down Vallecito Creek, up Johnson Creek and over Columbine Pass, and down to Needleton and the railroad. This trip would consume a week for a strong party (it should not be attempted by others), and two weeks would be needed if much climbing was done or many side trips taken.

Needleton-Webb Lake—8 miles; 2900 feet. Webb Lake, shown but not labelled on the U.S.G.S. map, is approached by a good trail which begins about 2 miles up Needle Creek, near an old water wheel. Fishing and camping at this and the two other lakes mentioned below are good. Families wanting a short backpack might camp at Needle Creek at the base of this trail, making side trips up to Webb, Pearl, Emerald, and Chicago Basin. Return by the same trail.

Needleton-Pearl Lake—10 miles; 3500 feet. Continue up the same trail and drainage from Webb Lake. Day hikes can be made from Pearl to the top of Overlook Point above. Return by the same trail.

Needleton-Emerald Lake—11 miles; 4300 feet. The trail to Emerald Lake goes over a low pass to the east of Pearl Lake, and a return trip can be made the same way. The old mining trail shown on the U.S.G.S. map to Emerald from Needle Creek has deteriorated, but it could be used for the return trip to make a circuit.

Needleton-Chicago Basin—14 miles; 3000-4500 feet. This beautiful bowl, situated beneath a circle of 14,000-foot peaks, is the natural destination for backpackers coming up Needle Creek. The trail is good, and there are good campsites at around 11,000 feet. There are fine lakes high in the Basin, at 12,500 feet, and day trips may also be made up to Columbine Pass. Some of the surrounding peaks are easy walking when the snow has melted off, but those planning on climbing many of the peaks will need mountaineering skills and tools. Return by the same route.

Vallecito Campground-Chicago Basin—36 miles; 6500 feet. Good trails cover this long route from the roadhead into Chicago Basin, but considerable snow should be expected well into July and sometimes August, since Columbine Pass is at 12,700 feet. Take the Vallecito Creek Trail 11½ miles to Johnson Creek. If Vallecito is too high to ford, stay on the west side after the bridge a couple of miles below Johnson Creek. The trail to Columbine Lake and Pass goes up Johnson Creek and then drops down into Chicago Basin.

SANGRE DE CRISTO RANGE

The Sangre de Cristo Range forms the Front Range, the first major uplift rising out of the Great Plains, in the southern part of Colorado and the northern end of New Mexico. The crest of the range does not form a part of the Continental Divide, which at this latitude lies far to the west. This is not because the Front Range is lower here than it is farther north, however. There are more peaks exceeding 14,000 feet in the Sangre de Cristo Range than in the northern part of the state where the Front Range forms the Divide.

The Colorado section of the Sangre de Cristo Range forms a high line running south and slightly east between the Great Plains on one side and the San Luis Valley on the other. The San Luis Valley forms a wide, fairly flat park between the Sangre de Cristos and the San Juans. A range of hills known as the Wet Mountains sits between the high peaks and the plains.

Sangre de Cristo means "Blood of Christ," and it is thought to refer to the colors shed on the range by the sun, when it is low in the sky. It is a beautiful and impressive chain of mountains.

The section of the range in Colorado which is included here centers around the Crestones, two of the more spectacular of Colorado's 14,000-foot peaks, which stand above the South Colony lakes. The area is administered by San Isabel and Rio Grande National Forests.

Approaches

The Crestones can be reached from either the plains side or the San Luis Valley, but the trails covered here come in from the east. Westcliffe, which is shown on the accompanying map, is most easily reached by taking Colorado State Route 96 west from Interstate 25 at Pueblo, south of Denver and Colorado Springs. At Westcliffe, turn south on State Route 69 for 3 or 4 miles and turn onto Schoolfield Road or Colfax Lane, depending on which approach you are using.

The area can be reached from the south by turning off on State 69 by Walsenburg, on Interstate 25 about 50 miles north of the New Mexico border. If crossing the mountains from the west, 69 turns south from U.S. 50 30 miles east of Salida. A county road goes north to Gardner, on 69, just before La Veta Pass, on U.S. 160 east of Alamosa and Fort Garland.

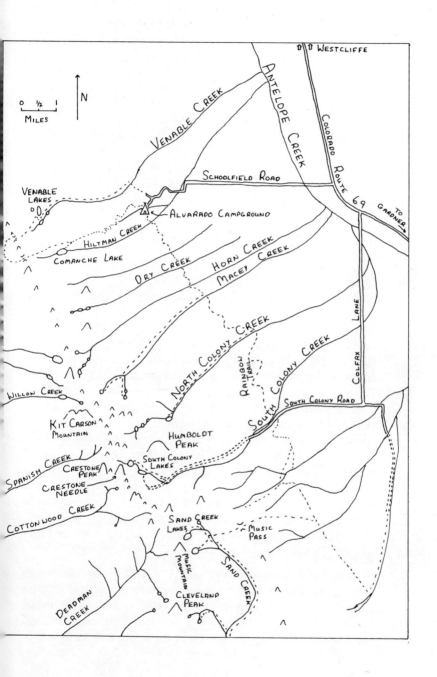

Campgrounds

The Forest Service only has one campground in this area, though there are other suitable campsites. To reach the Alvarado Campground, take State Route 69 3½ miles south of Westcliffe, turn right on Schoolfield Road, and continue for 5 miles until the road to the campground turns off to the left. There are 44 campsites.

Those planning trips that begin from South Colony Road, mentioned below, can find campsites along the road, on South Colony Creek, or along the Rainbow Trail.

Hikes

There are a number of good hikes starting from the campground, and there are good walks into the main peaks from South Colony Road. As shown on the map, this road turns right from Colfax Lane, which leaves Route 69 a little past Schoolfield Road. The road is good for a way up South Colony Creek before deteriorating to a jeep road. The quality of this road varies a good deal. Family automobiles can usually be driven easily for the first 3 or 4 miles of the 8 from Colfax Lane to the end of the road, only a mile or so from the lowest of the South Colony lakes. The rest of the road is sometimes passable to skilled drivers in Volkswagens, pickups, and other good backroad vehicles, but don't try going much beyond the intersection with the Rainbow Trail unless you have the skill and equipment for handling poor road conditions.

The hike up the remainder of South Colony Road takes one into the spectacular area of the South Colony lakes, and it is well worthwhile if one does not mind possible vehicular company. The other trails listed are less popular, however, and they will get the hiker away from the crowds quickly enough.

Rainbow Trail—various distances. The Rainbow Trail contours along the base of the range, making for pleasant walks through the woods, as well as connecting with trails following various creeks up to the high country. It can be used for short hikes from either the campground or the South Colony Road.

Comanche Lake—8 miles; 2700 feet. The trail to Comanche Lake starts directly upstream from the Alvarado Campground, later working south into the next watershed, and finally climbing to this pretty alpine-zone lake. Return the same way, or make the circuit discussed below. Map: Horn Peak, 7½′.

Venable Lakes—8 miles; 3000 feet. From the Alvarado Campground, follow the Rainbow Trail north ½ mile, past Abbot's Lodge, to the trail up Venable Creek. This pleasant group of four lakes is located in a cirque below Spring Mountain. The two lower lakes are in the trees and make good campsites. Return the same way, or make the circuit discussed below. Map: Horn Peak, 7½′.

Comanche Lake-Venable Lakes Circuit—13 miles; 4000 feet. This circuit makes a nice scenic trip, taking the hiker over the range crest briefly, with good views of the higher peaks to the south. Take the Venable Lakes trail, and continue to follow it uphill, past both the lower and upper lakes, contouring south around the cirque to a pass at about 12,700 feet. The trail then continues along the south side of the crest at the same elevation, crossing back over another pass after less than a mile, and dropping down into the cirque above Comanche Lake. Follow the Comanche Lake Trail back down to the campground. Maps: Horn Peak, 7½′; Electric Peak, 7½′.

Backpacking Trips

FROM ALVARADO CAMPGROUND:

Macey Lakes—18 miles; 3000 feet. This fine little group of lakes is nested below somewhat more rugged peaks than Venable and Comanche. There are good campsites, and the spot is not much visited. Take the Rainbow Trail southeast from Alvarado campground for 5½ miles, and then follow the trail up Macey Creek to the lakes. Return the same way. Maps: Horn Peak, 7½′; Crestone Peak, 7½′.

North Colony Lakes—24 miles; 5000 feet. The North Colony lakes are closer to the major 14,000-foot peaks of the area than some of the other spots listed, yet they see far fewer visitors than the South Colony lakes. They are below the north side of Humboldt, which is far more interesting than its southern exposure, and a climb to the Humboldt saddle will give the hiker spectacular views of the Crestones to the south and Kit Carson to the west. Take the Rainbow Trail southeast from the campground 10 miles to North Colony Creek, and then follow the trail up the creek to the lakes. A day should be allowed for exploring the upper lakes and beyond, which mileage and elevation gain is not included in the preceding figures. To reach the Humboldt saddle, continue past the third large lake and head up the relatively gentle slope west of the peak. (This is a snow slope early in the season.) Humboldt is an easy climb from the saddle. Maps: Horn Peak, 7½'; Crestone Peak, 7½'

FROM SOUTH COLONY ROAD:

North Colony Lakes—15 miles; 3000 feet. From its intersection with South Colony Road, take the Rainbow Trail north 4½ miles to North Colony Creek, and follow the trail up the creek to the lakes. See the description above for more information on the lakes. Maps: Horn Peak, 7½'; Crestone Peak, 7½'; Beck Mountain, 7½'.

North Colony Lakes-South Colony Lakes Circuit—14 miles; 3500 feet. This fine circuit involves some cross-country travel, but it is not exceptionally difficult once the spring snow is melted. Follow the trail up to the North Colony lakes. Continue past the third large lake and climb up the slope of Humboldt Peak to the saddle. A side trip from here to the top of Humboldt will require an extra mile of travel and an extra 1200 feet of climbing; return to the saddle if the climb of Humboldt is made. From the saddle work carefully down the slopes to the head of

A 14,000-foot peak in the Colorado Rockies rises forbiddingly above the beautiful lakes at its foot. The Crestone Needle.

the South Colony Lake cirque below. (Do not attempt this descent on snow slopes unless you have an ice ax and experience; snow in early season is steeper on this side than on the North Colony side.) From the South Colony lakes follow the trail down to the jeep road and thence back to the car. Maps: Horn Peak, 7½′; Crestone Peak, 7½′; Beck Mountain, 7½′.

CHAPTER 10

Trips in New Mexico

SANGRE DE CRISTO RANGE

THE SANGRE DE Cristo Range (the name means "Blood of Christ") extends from southern Colorado well into New Mexico, and it includes the highest mountains in New Mexico, as well as the high country which is most alpine in character. As in Colorado, this is a front range, rising to its great height from the edge of the plains. The mountains are administered by Carson and Santa Fe National Forests and lie to the east of the cities of Taos and Santa Fe.

The area shown is at the headwaters of the Pecos River, east of Santa Fe, in the southern part of the range. The highest peak is Santa Fe Baldy, 12,622 feet.

Approaches

Interstate 25 coming to Santa Fe from the northern states loops south around the Sangre de Cristos so that it actually comes into the city from the southeast. Take one of the exits for Pecos from this road (20 miles from Santa Fe if one is coming from the city; 28 miles out if one is driving from the direction of Colorado). From Pecos, continue north into the mountains on New Mexico State Route 63. Cowles, which is shown on the map, is about 18 miles north of Pecos.

Campgrounds

There are three Forest Service campgrounds convenient to the trails discussed here. The hikes described leave from Winsor Creek Campground, which has 7 campsites and is located a mile west of Cowles. Holy Ghost Campground is equally convenient to the trails, as shown on the map, merely adding a round-trip distance of 2 miles to any of the hikes listed. It is 2 miles northwest on a Forest Service road which leaves State Route 63 5 miles south of Cowles (13 miles north of Pecos), and has 22 sites. Panchuela Campground, with 6 sites, is 1½ miles north of Cowles. There are also other Forest Service campgrounds, not shown, to the north and northeast of Cowles.

Hikes

Stewart Lake—6 miles; 1850 feet. Take the trail up Winsor Creek from the campground. The short side trail to Stewart Lake turns uphill to the right after 2½ miles. Map: Cowles, 7½ '.

Lake Katherine—9 miles; 3400 feet. This lovely little lake is nestled just under Santa Fe Baldy. It makes a beautiful campsite if this hike is used for a backpacking trip; it is open enough for a fine view, but there are enough trees for a nice camp. Fishing is good. Take the trail up Winsor Creek to its head at the lake. Maps: Cowles, 7½ ', Aspen Basin, 7½ '.

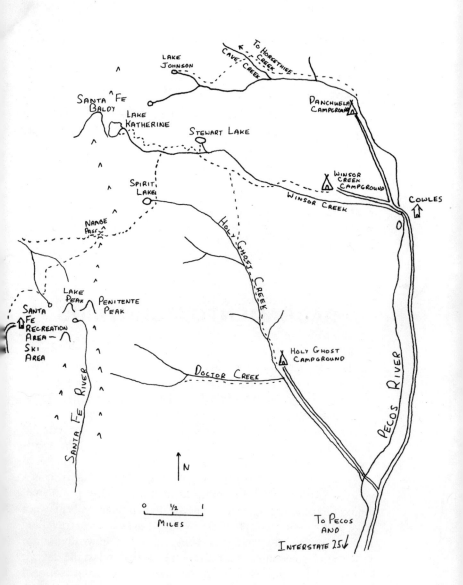

Lake
Johnson

To Horsethief
Creek

Cave Creek

Panchuela
Campground

Santa Fe
Baldy

Lake
Katherine

Stewart Lake

Winsor
Creek
Campground

Cowles

Spirit
Lake

Winsor Creek

Nambe
Pass

Holy Ghost Creek

Lake
Peak

Penitente
Peak

Santa
Fe
Recreation
Area —
Ski
Area

Holy Ghost
Campground

Doctor Creek

Santa Fe River

Pecos River

N

0   ½   1
MILES

To Pecos
And
Interstate 25

Spirit Lake—9 miles; 2000 feet. About ¾ mile beyond the cutoff for Stewart Lake, the Winsor Trail leaves the creek, contouring south to Spirit Lake. Maps: Cowles, 7½′, Aspen Basin, 7½′.

Backpacking Trip

Santa Fe Baldy—12 miles; 4600 feet. Take the trail to Spirit Lake. Continue up the trail to a saddle (Nambe Pass) and then follow the ridge north to the peak. Those with energy to spare can also go south along the crest to Penitente and Lake Peaks, above the Santa Fe Recreation Area, adding another 3 miles to the trip. Another way to do the climb is to backpack to Lake Katherine and camp there, climbing Baldy directly from the lake. It is a 1000-foot climb, largely on scree and with no trail. Maps: Cowles, 7½′, Aspen Basin, 7½′.

SACRAMENTO MOUNTAINS

The Sacramento Mountains give a good introduction to the character of the Rockies in southern New Mexico. They are higher than most, with Sierra Blanca Peak, which is shown on the accompanying map, rising to 12,000 feet, high enough to collect a reasonable amount of snow. This group thus rises high enough to be less arid than some of the surrounding ranges, and the access roads are good enough not to require any special attention.

Though this is not really a desert range of mountains, it is a good deal drier than the Rockies further north. Most people will enjoy it most in spring or fall. The smaller campgrounds may not have water, so it is wise to carry plenty in the car when travelling in this country. Many of the canyons and creeks shown do not run year-round, so enough water should be carried to last the day.

Most of the area shown on the map is in Lincoln National Forest, but to the south the land belongs to the Mescalero

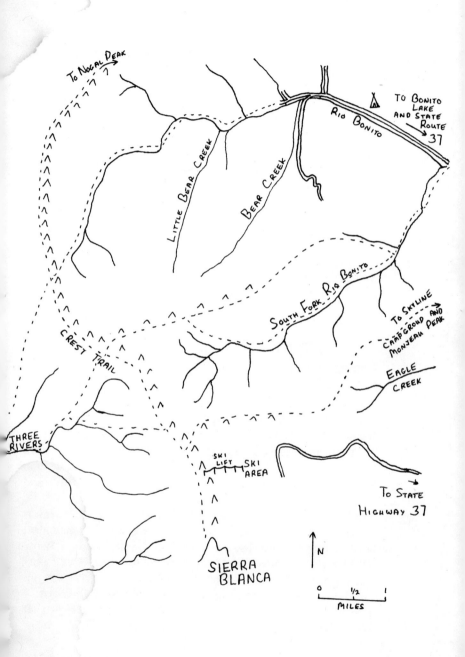

Apaches who run the ski area shown on the map. They also have a number of campgrounds, lakes, and recreation facilities in the area. The route shown into the mountains in this book goes through the National Forest, but there are also a number of trails from the Reservation. If you choose to use the Indians' land, you will be expected to pay reasonable fees—this is one of the Apaches' main sources of revenue. Special fishing permits are required for the lakes and reservoirs on tribal land, in addition to a New Mexico license.

Approaches

If Interstate 25 is taken south from Albuquerque, take U.S. 380 east, 11 miles beyond Socorro. After 66 miles, U.S. 54 is crossed, and after about another 20 miles New Mexico Route 37 goes off to the right. Take route 37 past Nogal, and turn right on the road to Bonito Lake. New Mexico 37 is also reached from the south by leaving U.S. 70 at Ruidoso. The turnoff for Lake Bonito is about 9 miles north.

Campgrounds

In addition to the Forest Service campgrounds mentioned here, there are a number of private campgrounds near Ruidoso, and the Mescalero Apaches have several on the way north from Ruidoso.

From the turnoff to Lake Bonito, the South Fork Campground with 60 campsites is 4 miles. The trail system shown continues beyond it, and there are additional trails and interesting ruins up most of the side canyons.

Another campground giving access to the trail system is Skyline Campground, reached by a road going west and then northwest from Alto, itself 5 miles north of Ruidoso on Route 37. Skyline is 4 miles from Alto, near the Monjeau Peak Lookout. It has 17 campsites, suitable for tents only.

Other Forest Service campgrounds nearby are Oak Grove, 4 miles west of Alto with 31 tent sites, and Cedar Creek, just off 37 a mile north of Ruidoso, with 37 tent sites.

Spring fills the lower altitudes with new growth, and the evergreen forests that cover the lower elevations in the Rockies are fresh and inviting.

Hikes

For short walks, pick any of the trails going up side canyons off Rio Bonito. There are roads or jeep tracks up a number of them, but most of these narrow down to foot trails after a while. Where private land is posted, respect the signs. There are a good many private holdings here.

The best views of the region are from the trail along the crest of the Range, which runs all the way from Nogal Peak to Sierra Blanca Peak.

Rio Bonito Road to Crest—9 miles; 2000 feet. Follow the trail up Rio Bonito Canyon to the crest and return.

Rio Bonito Road to Crest Circuit—14 miles; 2600 feet. Head up to the crest as in the preceding hike, and turn south along the crest trail for 1½ miles to a side trail leading east along a ridge dividing the Rio Bonito Canyon from the South Fork Canyon. Take this trail down.

Sierra Blanca Peak from Rio Bonito—18 miles; 5000 feet. Take the trail up the South Fork Rio Bonito to the crest, and follow the trail south to the peak. Return the same way.

Sierra Blanca Peak from Skyline Campground—16 miles; 3200 feet. Take the trail along the ridge from Skyline Campground to the crest and continue 1½ miles to the peak. Return by the same route.

Backpack Trip

Rio Bonito to Three Rivers Circuit—18 miles; 5000 feet. Take the trail up the main Bonito Canyon to the crest. Just to the south a canyon goes down on the other side of the crest. Follow the trail down this canyon to the main Three Rivers Canyon. To return, head up either of the trails which work west up to the crest, and take the South Fork Rio Bonito trail down. A side trip to the top of Sierra Blanca Peak will add 6 miles to the trip.